T0049987

"Chris and Laura Smith take their decades of experience in both ministry and the marketplace and walk you through the discovery process of your unique giftings, leaving no question in your mind as to why God put you here. *Make Your Splash* is an energizing, mobilizing read!"

Dr. Robert Jeffress, pastor, First Baptist Church, Dallas

"I wish I had read this book many years ago—I have struggled in my life, failed at times, and learned many lessons in trying to understand what my God-given gifts truly are and how to use them. So now, instead of having to learn how to take care of your eyes by yourself, you are now offered help from two great 'eye doctors.'"

Ming Wang, Harvard and MIT (M.D.), Ph.D. (laser physics); director, Wang Vision Institute, Nashville

"Chris and Laura Smith have offered practical, applicable advice on how to share the love of Jesus in a military and paramilitary environment, or in any environment or industry you are called to."

Richard Travis DeLano, district fire chief, LCFD

"Chris and Laura Smith are well-known and respected, and their family is also known for their varied talents and impressive creativity in worship and in work. This book's theme of the quest for self and fitting into our world as a part of God's design—great thoughts for all."

Randy Atkins, Chick-fil-A owner/operator and former employer of several Smiths

"An inspirational guide to finding and flowing to your personal path of purpose. Chris and Laura have created a new lens to view your unique gifts and go make what only you can."

Lea Little, TV host, Amazon influencer, lifestyle entrepreneur

MAKE
YOUR
splash

MAKE YOUR *splash*

Maximize Your Career and Cultural Impact by Discovering Your Spiritual Personality

LAURA HARRIS SMITH AND CHRISTOPHER LEE SMITH

Chosen
a division of Baker Publishing Group
Minneapolis, Minnesota

© 2023 by Laura H. Smith and Christopher Lee Smith

Published by Chosen Books
Minneapolis, Minnesota
www.chosenbooks.com

Chosen Books is a division of
Baker Publishing Group, Grand Rapids, Michigan

Printed in the United States of America

All rights reserved. No part of this publication may be reproduced, stored in a retrieval system, or transmitted in any form or by any means—for example, electronic, photocopy, recording—without the prior written permission of the publisher. The only exception is brief quotations in printed reviews.

Library of Congress Cataloging-in-Publication Data
Names: Smith, Laura Harris, author. | Smith, Christopher Lee, author.
Title: Make your splash : maximize your career and cultural impact by discovering
    your spiritual personality / Laura Harris Smith and Christopher Lee Smith.
Description: Minneapolis, Minnesota : Chosen Books, a division of Baker
    Publishing Group, [2023] | Includes bibliographical references.
Identifiers: LCCN 2022047580 | ISBN 9780800799199 (trade paper) | ISBN
    9780800763176 (casebound) | ISBN 9781493439898 (ebook)
Subjects: LCSH: Vocation—Christianity. | Professions—Religious aspects—
    Christianity. | Vocational guidance. | Christian life.
Classification: LCC BV4740 .S64 2023 | DDC 248.4—dc23/eng/20221115
LC record available at https://lccn.loc.gov/2022047580

Unless otherwise indicated, Scripture quotations taken from the (NASB®) New American Standard Bible®, Copyright © 1960, 1971, 1977, 1995 by The Lockman Foundation. Used by permission. All rights reserved. www.lockman.org

Scripture quotations identified NASB2020 taken from the (NASB®) New American Standard Bible®, Copyright © 1960, 1971, 1977, 1995, 2020 by The Lockman Foundation. Used by permission. All rights reserved. www.lockman.org

Scripture quotations identified ESV are from The Holy Bible, English Standard Version® (ESV®), copyright © 2001 by Crossway, a publishing ministry of Good News Publishers. Used by permission. All rights reserved. ESV Text Edition: 2016

Scripture quotations identified NIV are from THE HOLY BIBLE, NEW INTERNATIONAL VERSION®, NIV® Copyright © 1973, 1978, 1984, 2011 by Biblica, Inc.® Used by permission. All rights reserved worldwide.

Scripture quotations identified NKJV are from the New King James Version®. Copyright © 1982 by Thomas Nelson. Used by permission. All rights reserved.

Cover design by LOOK Design Studio

All images from Shutterstock.com

Baker Publishing Group publications use paper produced from sustainable forestry practices and post-consumer waste whenever possible.

23   24   25   26   27   28   29   7   6   5   4   3   2   1

To Eastgate Creative Christian Fellowship:

For the last twenty years of Sundays you have afforded your
pastors the creative liberty to dream, innovate and develop our
enterprising ideas in real time for you. This book is one of them!

There is no other church like you, Eastgate, and we love you.

Contents

Contents

Part Three Turn the Tide   233

(In this third part you will make some applications that will help you get in the flow of your particular river.)

Foreword

Every generation must be willing to seek God for an expansion of understanding and revelation for the hour in which they live. As Bishop Bill Hamon says, "There is no new truth, only restored truth." This flows into his definition of what he calls the saints movement. This is the last of a series of biblical restorations found in Ephesians 4:10–12. According to Bishop Hamon, the 1950s saw restoration of the office of the evangelist, the '60s, the pastor, the '70s, the teacher, the '80s, the prophet, the '90s, the apostle, and then with the turn of the 21st century, the saints movement.

In each season of restored truth, meaning that it was there all the time, it was just not seen except by a few forerunners or early adopters. Restoration truths, however, become more main-streamed throughout whole movements as they are taught. This is when the understanding moves beyond the initial early-adopter stage to mid- or even late-adopter stage.

The revelation that God has given five offices—apostle, prophet, pastor, teacher and evangelist—is coming of age, as it were, for this time. But what about the saints? Do they have a part in being apostolic, prophetic and so forth? Chris and Laura Smith say yes!

Ephesians 4:12 says the offices are for the equipping of the saints. This word *equipping*, in the Greek, literally means to "set a bone in order." Ephesians 4:4 says there is one body and one Spirit.

Could it be that in order to see the full measure of the restoration of the saints, we need to expand our thinking to understand that each believer also has a job to do in order to see the full equipping of the Body of Christ? This in no way negates the fact that God has anointed those who will equip through their fivefold offices.

How are we to see the full restoration needed to see God's will be done on earth as it is in heaven, without attributes of who He is also being distributed broadly through what Chris and Laura have called the twelve rivers? Each sphere of society needs the power of God specifically flowing through it.

Chris and Laura Smith are not novices to biblical truth. They are pastors of a very creative and wonderful church and students of the Word. Please read this book with an open mind and prayerful heart. It is a pioneering work, and I encourage you to seek the Holy Spirit on how He would have you implement it. Now, open the pages and dive into *Make Your Splash*.

Cindy Jacobs, co-founder, Generals International, Dallas, Texas

I'm not adept at writing book forewords and would hesitate to do so, but I'm pretty good with relationships and have known Chris and Laura Smith for many years. The insight and creativity I have observed in this couple have always seemed remarkable to me. So since they have been willing to take the time, as a couple, to lay out what might be some really fresh concepts for your future success, I would suggest this book for you.

Mike Jacobs, co-founder, Generals International, Dallas, Texas

PART ONE

Test the Waters

Goals

1. For you to hear about the origin of the twelve rivers concept and find your purpose
2. For you to revisit the multiple times God has used water to perform miracles
3. For you to discover your "net worth" through your natural and acquired gifts
4. For you to review the world's top 20 personality tests and what they reveal
5. For you to learn the five personality types of God and test yourself to discover which of those most flows through you.

Just Add Water

Are you sitting down? What I mean is, are you sitting, standing or reclining? The answer is actually none of the above, because despite the stationary position you think you are currently in, the truth is that you are moving. Fast. And no, I'm not describing the earth's rotational pull that would cause constant physical acceleration were it not for the laws of gravity upon your body. You see, your very life itself is in a current that is flowing in a decided direction, a direction determined by you alone. And even if you believe that your life course is being entirely dictated by a divine force, you can at least admit that you have the free will to mess around and get lost, or to stay on course. So in that sense, you are responsible for the movement of your life. You belong to the present time, but you are moving steadily toward a future that God has created just for you. And guess what . . . He is already there! With Him in front of you and Chris and me behind you, cheerleading you on, you are sure to arrive in perfect time.

As a naturopathic doctor, I enjoy helping people get healthy—body, mind and spirit. But I also enjoy helping them figure out why they were born. So does my husband, Chris. As pastors, we do not claim to have the power to hand out destinies, but we do observe people, their skills and their passions, and we often offer course correction in order to help steer folks in what we perceive to be the right direction for their lives. God gave us such an opportunity in the late winter/early spring of 2021, as we found ourselves encouraging a church full of our people who were wondering if they had just lost a full year of their lives to a global pandemic. Mind you, they are a faith-filled bunch at Eastgate Creative Christian Fellowship near Nashville, Tennessee, but many were asking themselves questions like, *What was last year even about? Did I lose ground—physically, emotionally and spiritually? How do I get it back? Will this year be any different or better for me?*

As 2021 stretched into another year that seemed a carbon copy of the one before it, with so many still in isolation, recovery or both, people were forced to think hard about their lives. Forced to lock down, they began to look up and reimagine life. Entrepreneurs were born. Homeschooling parents were born. And of course, literal children were born. At Eastgate, shortly after the national lockdowns, we had a baby boom that tripled our previous church record of babies born in a single year. Suddenly, this question was nagging us all: *Was this worldwide Pause button a mechanism that might provide me with the ability to reinvent myself and create a brand-new life, or will I just press Play on the old one once this is all over?*

These are just some of the questions that people were asking at Eastgate. Maybe you were asking them, too.

Your Piece

So, in February 2021 we started an eight-week sermon series entitled "Awaken Your Piece," focusing on helping people discover the "piece" (their gifts, talents, contributions) that they could bring to this "new" world. To look upon the world scene like a giant puzzle and see the gaping hole that is just waiting for your piece to be dropped in. We had been praying all winter at Eastgate for another Great Awakening—believing that the "woke world" was a counterfeit for such a global awakening—and by spring we were coming to the conclusion that a worldwide awakening must simply just be a collection of little personal awakenings. We imagined a whole world full of people awakening to their individual purposes and then plugging them into society, and Chris and I decided we could at least be responsible for *our* church experiencing such an awakening. We never dreamed that those next two months at Eastgate would give birth to a movement . . . this book, spin-off videos, commissioning services, testing material, television specials, merchandise and more.

This book is a crash course in what Eastgate members experienced in those two months. Jehovah Sneaky gave us a sweet gift just as the sting of winter was leaving and the last snow was melting, and as green was starting to bud on the trees all around us. It was as if nature was awakening on the outside as we were awakening on the inside.

Chris actually took the first four Sundays in the series, and I didn't even step in until weeks five and six. His spirit was so full that he inspired people for a month straight and most definitely "awakened" them to the idea that they were each created for a specific purpose. That means that the piece I brought to the series—which was the fun and playful concept of the rivers—had not even dropped into my spirit yet. Keep that in mind as I describe these first four Sundays to you, because they stand on their own as incredible revelation that God gave Chris about how He wants to partner with *you* on earth to accomplish great things. Things, in fact, that God simply cannot do without you!

To be honest, I think I expected on week one for Pastor Hubby to tell us all to take a typical spiritual gift test and then to study the Ephesians 4 "fivefold ministry" passage to get an idea of how God gets things done in the earth. Instead, Chris laid out a beautiful, relational picture of what he calls the five personalities of God, which you will read all about in chapter 6. You can actually go to the YouTube Eastgate Creative Christian Fellowship channel and watch the whole series, although the teaching has evolved since then. Just scroll down to the "Awaken Your Piece" playlist and you will see the entire series.

We also decided to share the eight-week series teaching duties with our son, Jhason, who is Eastgate's associate pastor, along with his wife, Brittany. But first, their son would teach us something. If you watch the series on YouTube, you will notice that on the first Sunday that Chris spoke, our then two-year-old grandson and Jhason's oldest, Jadwin, spoke into the microphone a two-word message that would sum up Papa's (his grandfather's) upcoming sermon, and in many ways this whole book (at minutes 44:24–46:20). In a kids' movie Jad liked at the time, one of the main characters felt purposeless. The character even said she had "no purpose." Jad's parents didn't want him to have that concept left in his head, so instead of saying "no purpose," they began teaching him to say, "yes, purpose!" With his mama's help (a very pregnant Brittany), a two-year-old child inspired us that Sunday at Eastgate with those two words—to remember that yes, we had a purpose, too.

Three days later, Brittany gave birth to their second son, and she and Jhason began their paternity/maternity leave. At the same time, I was finishing up writing *Give It to God and Go to Bed* (Chosen, 2021), with a looming deadline. It was a good thing God had inspired Chris to speak for a month of Sundays! Having taught on the five personalities of God, he then spent a couple of weeks discussing the ways of God, using Galatians 5 as a very practical springboard to describe how the nine gifts of the Spirit manifest themselves in each of these distinct five personalities.

By the way, let me just say from the start that we are in no way implying that God has multiple personalities or some sort of multiple personality disorder. Just think of these "five personalities" like five personas, or five traits or attributes of God that play out in your own God-given personality. If anything, this ideology that we are about to roll out for you brings incredible order to the Body of Christ, and of course, purpose! It is so practical. You are going to love chapter 9, as you discover which of the five personalities primarily flows through you. This discovery will both help you reach others with the Good News of Jesus Christ *and* help you stop comparing yourself to the way others do that. Let everybody else be what God created them to be. You do you.

My Turn

March came, and it was my turn to add my perspective to the series. I felt led to bring in the piece of finding your purpose in the workplace and how you could actually make a living with the gifts of God within you, while also making maximum impact for God. Immediately, I thought of the "Seven Mountains of Influence" teaching, an incredibly powerful and popular concept that originated with Loren Cunningham (Youth With a Mission— YWAM) and Bill Bright (Campus Crusade for Christ) in 1975, and has gone on to be expounded upon by insightful authors such as Lance Wallnau and Johnny Enlow. (And perhaps we should give original honor to Bishop Bill Hamon, who long before that was urging the Church to get out of its four walls and impact culture for Jesus Christ.) The mountains concept is one that basically says the world is molded by seven main facets of society, and that the influence you are able to have in society will happen in one of those seven spheres. Each sphere is symbolized by a mountain on which God wants to place you occupationally and use you for His ultimate glory.

The seven mountains are education, religion, family, business, government, arts/entertainment and media. Champions of the seven mountain idea propose that culture is most impacted by these seven industries, not to mention that by working in them you can also have maximum influence in the earth. This is a fascinating concept that has been criticized by some as being an agenda by which Christians are scheming to attain global domination. Some detractors even go so far as to say it suggests that Christ cannot return until we accomplish this domination. But I don't see that as the heart behind this concept at all. And its message is turnkey enough that I immediately thought of it as a means by which to introduce my portion of the Eastgate teaching series and inspire people not only to find out what their purpose is, but to use that information so naturally in their occupations that they would wonder if they were even working for a living. My father used to tell me, "Find something you love to do, and you'll never work a day in your life."

My plan was to have everyone stand up in the church at the very beginning and seat them according to what I felt their mountains would be (interviewing the visitors briefly from the stage and then sending them to their sections). I realized it would be a bit discombobulating for those who prefer to sit down, stay put and not engage much (which were a few more than normal due to social distancing). Yet knowing what a flexible bunch of eager learners we have at Eastgate, I figured it was a safe place to conduct such an experiment. But boy, was I in for a big surprise as I sat preparing the night before. With the church database pulled up in front of me, I suddenly became aware of how many people in our congregation simply would not fit into one of the seven mountain categories. Most did, but what about the medical/health professionals? What about the engineers and scientists? They could plausibly be worked into one of those existing mountains, but didn't they deserve a mountain of their own since they have so much cultural impact? We had all of the above "extras" at Eastgate, and I was finishing up medical school to become a naturopathic doctor myself. So which mountain should I go scale?

I also saw another gaping hole that was not going to work for our church. By my initial guesstimates, a whopping 42 percent of our congregation should be on one mountain—the arts and entertainment mountain. Also, when I separated the quiet artists (painters, writers, textile workers) from the magnetic entertainers (actors, singers, performers), they were split 22 percent and 20 percent respectively. Their giftings were so different that it just didn't seem fitting to put them on the same mountain path.

At first, I decided that maybe I could add new "mountains." Not because I wanted to change this very God-inspired concept, but because very practically, it was crucial that everyone have a place to sit the next morning in church! And more importantly, it was crucial for everyone to have a place to fit in the world. I knew if I didn't figure something out, it would be embarrassing for the people who were standing around wondering where they fit in. They would get dumped into a miscellaneous category, not knowing where they belonged and how God could use them there. Still, I felt hesitant to alter this amazing seven mountain concept, even though countless spin-off books have been written and rewritten about it, and I wouldn't have been in any "trouble" for doing so.

God's Shift

Then about 1:00 a.m., as I considered that I really should be in bed so I could be clearheaded for the teaching, the Holy Spirit instructed me to shift the sermon completely. Trust me, I was *so* tired and wanted to call it a night *so* badly, but what happened next jarred me wide awake. I heard the following phrases in this order:

> *Rivers, not mountains, for your teaching.*

> *Mountains don't move, but rivers flow everywhere and touch everything.*

> *Mountains can be intimidating because they must be scaled; tell people to find their river and just go play in it.*

God impressed upon me certain concepts that revolved around a different approach to influencing culture. In no way does this undermine the seven mountain teaching (which I obviously respect and was planning to reference), but those are the phrases that I heard, and these are the questions that they begged:

> *How do you "find your river and go play in it," God?*

> *Do you just jump in from the steep bank?*

> *Or do you flow into it in the same way that rivers are made up of other smaller streams that empty into them?*

As the daughter (and now wife) of an avid fisherman, my mind was suddenly abuzz with river ideas, idioms and images! In the wee hours, I gathered online pictures and videos of running water as a backdrop to my sermon, in order to visually inspire the people with the life-changing advice I was about to deliver. I wanted them to see the water, and at times the audio even peeked through so they could hear the rushing waves. I exported it all into a 30-minute video to be played under the majority of my teaching. Just as a good soundtrack is important to any movie, I knew this soundtrack was important to this teaching that I then was calling "The Ten Cultural Rivers of Influence." (I didn't know yet that a couple more rivers were yet to rise.)

I wound up never going to bed at all that night, finally finishing the sermon as the sun came up, then rushing to get ready and get to the church to preach it. I was brimming with the energy that fresh revelation brings. It doesn't matter how tired, hungry or scattered you are when God wants to do a new thing and you think you are the first to know about it. You are suddenly sharp, satisfied and have no sense of self. I now had a shiny new revelation and one hour to try it out on a familiar audience. And you will see in chapter 7 how the rivers concept flowed perfectly (pun intended) with the previous month's theme of Chris's five personalities of God.

That morning, I stood everyone up and had them line the walls and even the back of the church. It was in the middle of a pandemic and we had about 40 percent of our people out, but you can watch the service on YouTube and see how I accomplished it. Perhaps it was a blessing that the crowd was smaller. With the database in hand, I called names and numbers and instructed people to sit in their designated sections. I didn't tell them why I was doing it or even mention the rivers yet. As for visitors, I did my best at placing them after a brief chat, or I just had some sit with the friend who had brought them until they knew which section they belonged in.

Their Reactions

The results? Everyone had a place that morning. No one was left out! We learned about each river, who belongs in it, and how you make your splash there. Some who were in certain occupations quickly learned that they were just doing their job to "pay the bills," and they wound up moving to another section to "stick their toe in the water" and see if God might be calling them to step out and use their gifts to influence culture from there instead. Sitting for an hour with kindred spirits was a good jump start for them, and very affirming for those veterans already sure of their callings.

The rivers concept was so well received that we planned a part 2 for the next Sunday, which wound up becoming a full-fledged commissioning service. Cultural influencers sat together again by group and lined up at the end to come through and have their hands washed by our pastors—in a water baptism of sorts—into a new calling, or an affirmation of the calling they were already living out. The week before, they had heard and seen the water as I taught. This time, they touched it. It was momentous! And it is the exact type of commissioning service that we recreated and filmed so that you might take your own church or company through a similarly beautiful experience by using the videos at the end of this book. Just add water!

Still glowing from the whole experience and all the positive feedback, that very afternoon as I was arriving home from church I got a text out of the blue from Carra Carr, my former director of marketing at Chosen Books. We had not even spoken since the year before, and that was only by text. She had dreamed about me in the middle of the night—at the same exact time that God was shifting my sermon theme from mountains to rivers—and she shared it with me. In her dream, I was sitting on a bench in between where two rivers met. We were in her hometown of Anoka, Minnesota. (The name *Anoka* is a combination of Dakota and Ojibwa words meaning respectively "on both sides" and "working waters," and locally they say it is "the place where two rivers meet," because the Mississippi River and the Rum River meet there.) Carra said I told her it was my favorite place to come, and we talked about a possible book (which you are now reading). I pointed out a cove farther down that I liked to visit in order to go deeper into the river, and I kept urging her to pray. Finally, she pointed out to me a familiar coffee shop nearby that was being modernized with a remodel. Then she woke up.

As you can imagine, I was shocked by Carra's text. I had even used the Mississippi River in the sermon (discussing how rivers often flow into oceans). I had also used the convergence of "two rivers" to symbolize how you can be in two occupational rivers at once. I knew that every bit of this confirmed that God was all over this idea. Carra eventually watched both sermons online and wrote back to say, "Laura, you *need* to publish this! It's powerful, prophetic and practical."

Within a week Chris and I left for a two-week vacation at . . . the beach. This trip to the water had been planned since the previous year, but now I viewed it through a whole new lens. I spent a lot of time thinking about water, watching water, experiencing water. While we were there, God expanded the ten rivers to twelve, speaking to me about the importance of our military and how they needed their own place, separate from the politicians on the government mountain. He also spoke to Chris about the service industry heroes and how waste management and restaurant workers have appointed destinies within their industries, too!

As I tip my hat and give my thanks to the many seven mountain pioneers, I believe that the piece in Carra's dream where she was showing me a familiar coffee shop remodel means that this new cultural rivers concept is merely a remodel of the familiar mountains theory. It is not a needless reinvention of coffee, but just a makeover of how and where it is served. It brings a user-friendly, playful way to find your calling and move in it.

This teaching should not feel heavy and serious. It should be completely natural and joyful! If it is not, then it will not be implemented. The world obviously is full of Christians who have no idea what God has called them to do, and who therefore are not doing it. We must figure out what our rivers of influence are and flow into them with ease. Once we get into the flow, we will learn other details about how we can swim against the current and shift culture. Chris and I will explore all the rivers with you in this book.

Our Role

Whether you are man or woman, black or white, rich or poor, tall or short, young or old, Christian or other, you have a river to discover. It is time to start flowing with God and moving toward your future.

In short, this book is for everyone. Because of that, Chris and I need to state (in case it has not already crossed your mind) that we did wonder if we had the governmental authority to introduce such a culture-shifting ideology to the entire Body of Christ. We certainly know we cannot fill the big shoes of spiritual fathers like Bill Hammond, Loren Cunningham or Bill Bright, even though we have our own shoes and leave our own footprints for others to follow in. But in light of that truth, we had to ask ourselves, *Well, then, why did God give this idea to us? Why did He just drop the rivers concept into the heart of a sleep-deprived shepherdess in the middle of a pandemic, in the middle of the night, just hours before it was to be tried out on a manageable, willing crowd?*

I mean, as stated at the beginning of this page, we are just pastors who love people and want to see them discover why they were born. So . . . we came to the conclusion that the reason God gave the idea to "just pastors" is because pastors have the role of being boots on the ground to see what is actually happening at the local church level. *In real time.* They assess the territory, organize the troops and educate the ranks. Therefore, I think we have our finger on the pulse of what is actually happening—and not happening—in the very Church itself. And we are deeply invested in seeing it thrive. When you say the word *church* to Chris and me, we don't see doctrines or facilities. We see people. Faces. Families. And we love them all. When they fail, we fail. When they hurt, we hurt. When they weep, we weep. But when they win, oh, how we win with them!

Chris and I invite you to join us on this river tour. You will hear from me in the odd-numbered chapters and Chris in the even-numbered ones. Our voices may sound different to you, but you will hear excitement in both of them. In part two you will learn your actual river (be patient!), but in this first part you will learn more about yourself—about your personality, and what God's personality looks like on you to the world. You will also come alive as you realize that you don't necessarily flow in the Spirit the way everyone else does, and shouldn't feel pressured to. If all of this is stirring you—and if you are perhaps a seven mountain fan—then here is your first move: *Just add water!*

Water is mentioned a total of 722 times in the Bible—more often than faith—so it is no surprise to us that God is still talking today about water. He also frequently used bodies of water in Scripture for miracles. In the next chapter, Chris is going to give you ten great New Testament examples to demonstrate just that. You will never view water the same.

The sound of water is worth more than all the poets' words.
Octavio Paz, twentieth-century Mexican poet and diplomat

2

There's Something in the Water

There *is* something in the water! We all love it. We all need it. And without it, we could not bodily survive more than three days. God created it for many practical reasons for life on earth. But there's more. In the first chapter, Laura outlined how the message for this book and movement started with a sermon, and then how, right before its delivery, God started talking to her about rivers and water. In this chapter, you will see the unique partnership God has with this vital element of His creation, water. It is a resource that not only sustains you physically, but a resource that embodies many spiritual significances that will prove essential for your spiritual life and purpose in the earth.

Water also has emotional benefits. Maybe you love a relaxing trip to the beach. I love trout fishing. I have tried pond fishing, lake fishing and even saltwater fishing, but there is nothing more exciting for me than fishing for rainbow, brook and brown trout in the running rivers of Middle and Eastern Tennessee. My river of choice is the Caney Fork River about fifty miles east of Nashville, in Smith County. The Caney Fork River is a watershed river for eleven counties in Middle Tennessee. It winds back and forth in a west/northwest direction along I-40, from Center Hill Dam and eventually into the Cumberland River. Known for its scenic landscapes and bountiful trout populations, the Caney Fork River is a popular retreat for people who enjoy fishing, kayaking, canoeing and hiking.

Rivers flow through mountain regions, through farmland, through rural communities, and eventually find their way into larger rivers that flow beautifully through metropolitan areas, with a final destination into our vast oceans. These springs, brooks, tributaries and rivers eventually connect to the oceans, even making the nations accessible through their intricate and confluent flow. Together, they form a network of life-giving and life-impacting influence on the cultures they uniquely touch.

Now, with that description in mind, think about your unique design, your unique gifts and talents. Think about those gifts and talents having the ability to flow through the various landscapes of your life. The people you meet, the place or places you work, the activities you enjoy and the relationships you possess. Your gifts and talents were given to you to enjoy, but they were also given to you in order for you to have a positive influence on those around you. That is the focus of this book. Laura and I want to inspire you not only to think about your natural abilities, but to discover the beautiful, God-given abilities you possess through Jesus and how they are to flow in the rivers of cultural impact in your life.

Let me share a top 10 list of examples from the New Testament that describes how Jesus flowed through the desert, mountain, rural and metropolitan regions of Israel in His day with God-given purpose to impact the lives of those around Him.

1. The baptism of Jesus—Matthew 3:1–17; Mark 1:1–11; Luke 3:15–22; John 1:19–34
2. Calming of the storm on the Sea of Galilee—Matthew 8:23–27; Mark 4:35–41; Luke 8:22–25

3. Two miraculous catches of fish—Luke 5:1–11; John 21:1–10
4. Jesus and Peter walk on the water—Matthew 14:22–36; Mark 6:45–56
5. The healing at the Pool of Siloam—John 9:1–12
6. Peter's taxes paid with a coin in a fish's mouth—Matthew 17:24–27
7. The woman at the well—John 4:1–42
8. Philip baptizes the Ethiopian eunuch—Acts 8:26–40
9. Paul's miracle at sea when shipwrecked on Malta—Acts 27
10. The beast, the woman and the river—Revelation 12:15–16

These are all interesting examples that directly involve water. Let's look at two of them more closely before we go on: the baptism of Jesus, and the healing of the blind man at the Pool of Siloam.

River Revival

Bethabara, or "Bethany beyond the Jordan," was a town located on the eastern bank of the Jordan River, just north of the Dead Sea, the lowest elevation on the face of the earth. It lay in stark contrast to the glorious Temple Mount, majestically nestled in the hills some 25 miles to the west. Bethany beyond the Jordan was a lowly place. It was not a place where the prominent or proud wanted to be seen. It was a place visited by those who were ready for a life transition. It was one of two primary baptism sites of John the Baptist.

As John preached "make straight the way of the Lord!" people eager for a life change made the humbling descent down and across the Kidron Valley to the Jordan River. The streets were buzzing with talk of John's preaching. There was growing anticipation over the revealing of the Messiah. Renewal was in the air. It was time for personal preparations to be made and priorities to be reset. The muddy waters of the Jordan began to fill up with the transgressions of the people being baptized, as John the Baptist, under the compulsion of the Holy Spirit, made his plea, saying, "Repent, for the kingdom of heaven is at hand" (Matthew 3:2).

Then one day, without warning, Jesus approaches the water's edge and stands before John. Impacted by His presence, John prophetically declares, "Behold, the Lamb of God" (John 1:29). Immediately, his tone turns from a voice of prophetic boldness to a voice of humble reverence at the sight of the Messiah, and he says, "I have need to be baptized by You, and do You come to me?" (Matthew 3:14). And Jesus answers him, "Permit it at this time; for in this way it is fitting for us to fulfill all righteousness" (verse 15). After Jesus is baptized, He comes up out of the water, the heavens open and John witnesses the Spirit of God descending from heaven in bodily form like a dove and remaining on Him. "And behold, a voice out of the heavens said, 'This is My beloved Son, in whom I am well-pleased'" (verse 17).

This location on the Jordan River is the same site where Israel entered into the Promised Land under Joshua's leadership. It is the same location where Elijah's miraculous chariot rode off into heaven. This area of the Jordan River has been called the place of transition or new beginnings because of these major biblical events. And now, as Jesus is raised up out of the muddy waters of the Jordan, another culture-impacting event takes place: the birth of the apostolic age under the leadership of the Messiah.

Like John the Baptist, you might feel unworthy of partnering with Jesus in fulfilling God's desire to see people come back into right standing with Him. If so, let this be a new beginning for you. Jesus came not only to save you, but to commission you into a life of service to God and His people. This is not a call into *the* ministry; it is a call simply to be available to minister to people right where you are and in the river(s) that God has purposed for your life.

Close your eyes right now and picture this: You are standing at a river. Jesus is coming to you and asking something from you. It is going to forever shape what others remember about you and will define the rest of your life and legacy. Say *yes* to Jesus and enter the river.

Sight Unseen

The Pool of Siloam was a ceremonial cleansing pool on the lower southern edge of the Temple Mount. The size of the *mikvah,* or pool, was so large that it was capable of accommodating hundreds of people at a time, with steps leading out of the water and up toward the Temple. It is believed that as Jews made their pilgrimage to Jerusalem for the holy days, they would go through the purification waters of the Pool of Siloam as they made their way up the Temple Mount to the Temple.

Running or living water was necessary for true cleansing and purification, according to Levitical Law. The water was a metaphor for the salvation of God. The running water that flowed into the Pool of Siloam came from the Gihon Spring to the east of the city, in the Kidron Valley, and was naturally siphoned up through tunnels that were carved out from underneath the city during King Hezekiah's reign. This sophisticated water system sent the water from the Gihon Spring to the pool so that the pool could continuously be filled with the living waters. *Gihon* means "to gush forth," and *Siloam* means "sent." It is a beautiful picture of how the salvation of God, the fountain of living waters that Jeremiah 2:13 talks about, will gush forth and flow inside us through Jesus, the Messiah.

As Jesus and His disciples were leaving the Temple, they saw a man who had been blind since birth. The young man was known by many in Jerusalem because he frequently sat outside the Temple and begged for money. It was presumed that his blindness and suffering were the result of sin, but Jesus quickly refuted His disciples' reasoning and told them that the man's condition "was so that the works of God might be displayed in him" (John 9:3).

How many times have you and I passed by someone in need of help? It is important to note that Jesus did not just pass by. He recognized a teachable moment for His disciples and an opportunity for the Kingdom of heaven to be advanced. He stopped, spat on the ground, made clay and wiped the man's eyes with it, and then told him to go wash in the Pool of Siloam. Think about that. Jesus told a blind man to walk downhill from the Temple Mount to the lower section of the city, where the pool was located. This would be about a 15-minute walk for the average person. Imagine the humiliation and faith it required of the blind man to have a complete stranger smear mud on his face, and then to agree to walk blind through the streets of Jerusalem on the Sabbath with dirt on his face. People must have been making a mockery of him. We know from Scripture that this event was the talk of the town. But he went away, washed, and came out of the water and headed back to the Temple *seeing*.

I wish I could have been a fly on the wall as the man made his way back up through the streets of Jerusalem to the Temple. The city was buzzing with speculation as people witnessed his amazing healing. The Pharisees were saying of Jesus, "This man is not from God, because He does not keep the Sabbath" (John 9:16). Yet under the grace and sensitivity of the Spirit, Jesus discerned, taught, cared for, commissioned and created an opportunity for the entire city of Jerusalem to hear the Good News of the Kingdom of heaven through this one encounter.

Now think about yourself and the journey you are on to find your own river, or to find purpose in the river in which you already belong. Laura and I want to help you get there. But you are going to help others while there, too. You are going to have your eyes opened to people who need help finding their purpose, and like Jesus, you will begin looking for those God encounters where you can lead them to their own river to experience their own water miracles.

So keep reading! But don't get too comfortable, because it is almost time to get out of the boat and set your eyes on Jesus as you walk upon your own river of influence. Laura and I are here to inspire you to do just that!

There are so many miracles documented in the entire Bible that portray water as a means by which God reveals Himself to His people and confirms Jesus as the Messiah. In the next chapter, Laura is going to show you examples of how God used water in the Old Testament to accomplish the impossible. There's something in the water, and God wants you to jump in and find that out for yourself.

> Water is the driving force in nature.
>
> Leonardo da Vinci, Renaissance-era
> Italian artist, inventor, engineer
> and architect

Waterworks

You probably noticed that Chris's New Testament water miracles list did not mention a few of the more popular phenomena, such as Jesus turning water into wine in John 2. Likewise, as I now turn my attention to Old Testament water marvels to remind you just how long God has been using water to reveal His purposes in the earth (and now in your life), you will notice that I exclude a few. Two examples are Moses striking the rock for it to produce water in Numbers 20, and Elijah dumping water on his offering to the Lord in front of the prophets of Baal in 1 Kings 18, before calling down fire from heaven that consumed his soggy sacrifice. Can you guess why we excluded these and other notable waterworks? Because as impressive as those miracles are, the ones we have chosen involved large bodies of water, so they best support our case for why God is drawing our attention to rivers right now.

Here is my top 10 list of miraculous examples from the Old Testament that all involve water:

1. The parting of the Red Sea in the Exodus (Exodus 14:1–31)
2. Elisha healing the water with the floating axe head (2 Kings 6:1–7)
3. Moses' basket survival story as a baby (Exodus 2:1–10)
4. The Nile becomes blood (Exodus 7:14–25)
5. Noah's Ark and the Great Flood (Genesis 6–9)
6. Naaman cleansed in the Jordan (2 Kings 5:1–14)
7. Jonah's experience at sea (the book of Jonah)
8. Rain stops through Elijah, and bodies of water dry up during drought (1 Kings 17:1–7)
9. Joshua and the crossing of the Jordan River (Joshua 3)
10. Ezekiel's experience of ankle-deep, knee-deep and waist-deep immersion in God (Ezekiel 47)

Of those ten, two have fascinated me since childhood: Noah and his Ark, and Ezekiel and his immersion in the river. Let's look at these two waterworks more closely.

MapQuest

I double-dog dare any engineer or architect out there to explain to me how Noah built the massive Ark using nothing but prehistoric tools. And explain how it served as a huge floating womb that safely protected eight people and countless animals, and how it delivered them onto dry ground yet never sprang a leak. Surely, that was the first miracle in this epic story. Either that, or the fact that Noah actually had the faith to take on such a project and to believe that the world was going to perish by flood, even though he himself had never seen rain!

That's right—many scientists believe that life on earth was sustained by nourishing dew and other subterrestrial bodies of water, and that up until the Flood, water had never come from the sky. So while these two chapters have been full of examples of how God utilized water for His people's deliverance and miraculous provision, think of how difficult it must have been for Noah to put his trust in this kind of watershed miracle, for two reasons: (1) he had never seen water fall from the sky to sustain life, and (2) he had never seen water flood the earth to destroy it. But he did believe, he did build and he was saved. Along with his three sons, without whom we would not be here today.

You heard me right: Every one of us can trace our roots back to either Shem, Ham or Japheth. Their father built the Ark, but then they built the world map. In the simplest terms, it can be said that when the waters receded and the Ark came to rest on Mount Ararat, Ham's people went on to head south into areas such as Ethiopia and Egypt; Japheth's family eventually moved westward and went on to become the European people, and then of course Americans; and Shem's people just stayed at the base of the mountain and became the Semites. And if you think of it, Israel has never tried to venture out and conquer the world or gain more territories. It has merely tried to stay right there at the base of that mountain and defend its own land against the anti-Semites.

In summation, thank God for rain, thank God for the Flood and thank God for how He baptized the earth, cleansed humankind and began again with a grace-drenched few to whom we all still owe our lives. Perhaps you need to get some of that pioneering perspective that Noah had when things get rough for you. Keep building! Stay afloat, even when the river floods! And most of all, remember that those who come after you will draw up maps and create new places, all because you stayed the course and didn't quit.

"Drownding" Down There

Ezekiel 47 shows us another example of how God used water to communicate to His people and bring revelation. If you don't know the story, then go read it, paying close attention to how God instructed Ezekiel in verses 3–5 to enter the water in increments as a symbol of Israel's coming advancements into its future. Ezekiel first enters into the water ankle deep, then knee deep, then waist deep, and then over his head. While Ez's prophetic act had nothing contextually to do with our lives today in this century, I do believe that we can greatly personalize it by comparing it to the level of faith we choose to walk in.

Instead of saying much more on this topic, I would merely like you to watch a video I made that echoes this analogy. It is a video of me stepping out into the Gulf of Mexico, right off Navarre Beach in the Florida Panhandle—ankle deep, then knee deep, then waist deep, until I was over my head—as a prophetic enactment of what abandoned faith feels like to me. You can find that uploaded video on my Facebook page at https://www.facebook.com/lauraharris-smith/videos/10159369726469136. And if you'll allow me to give another related personal example, I'd like to share with you what came to mind as soon as I typed the nickname Ez, which was what I once called my grandson, Ezra, when he was younger. When Ezra was about three years old, he almost drowned when he ventured out past all the adults and children in our private swim party at a relative's pool. That he was carried away by the undertow of a pool full of splashing, bouncing children is a better way to put it, and somehow he had wiggled out of his arm floaties, too.

I was not even supposed to be there that day because, to be frank, I don't like sitting by a pool and sweating half to death, nor do I like allowing chlorine to enter every pore of my body and harm it. But that morning, I had awakened to the voice of the Lord telling me to go. As you may have experienced, it was a still, inner voice and not an audible voice, but I knew it to be the voice of God from experience, so I reluctantly told Him I would go. When I asked why it was so important, He said, *Someone is going to drown there today unless you go.*

I found this hard to believe since I knew I wasn't going to be in the water, and I also knew I was probably the one with the least athletic ability and the poorest reflexes with which to be able to save anyone. But that day, as the wee ones and their outnumbered parents were in the shallow end and I was sitting all alone under the patio umbrella, watching the fun, my eye was drawn to some beautiful wildflower-type bushes. Since I was bored out of my skull, I decided to stroll over there and see if I could find a breeze near the beautiful shrubbery. I did, and when I turned around and looked over my left shoulder, there was Ezra, trying his best to hop back to safety on a rapidly slanting incline that was just too steep to provide any traction for his short little legs. He was not crying out for help—which I now see was because it was happening so fast and he likely didn't know what to expect or the danger that awaited him—and it was as his little head turned to-and-fro looking for help that our eyes met.

By the time I saw Ezra, the water was over his mouth and nose, and I saw his little eyes disappearing under the water line. Without a moment's notice I dove in fully dressed—$200 prescription sunglasses and all—and rescued him. I cannot quit crying right now, reliving it all. He choked and cried, and by that point, everyone saw what was happening and we got him to safety under the patio umbrella.

"Lollie, I was 'drownding' down there!" he said after we dried him off and I sat him on my lap. Someone snapped a picture right at that moment, and I am glad that they did because it reminds me to this day of how the voice of the Lord, and my reluctant "*sure, I'll go*" willingness to be interrupted by it, saved his little life. And may we all remember, the next time we are entering into new levels of faith—to the ankle, knees, waist and then head—that our God will never allow us to drown. Never!

This may even come to mind if you are led to step out into a new occupation after reading this book—a new river. Remember that He will not let you drown. Our advice in these pages should never override that of your spouse, pastor, parents or other people of authority in your life, of course. If you feel called to make drastic decisions and life changes after reading this book and taking its tests, by all means first run your thoughts by these wise people. Then, if there is unity and you get a green light from them, you can be sure of this: God will not let you get in over your head. God will never let you drown. And God *will* send help right when you need it.

So, friend, as we summarize this chapter and the one before it, reflecting on the many water marvels God has performed for His people, let me throw this marvel in to blow your mind: Not only is the earth made up of 75 percent water, but so is your body. That means your body instinctually responds to water, both naturally and supernaturally. Consider baptism. God did not choose a radical symbol of your profession of faith and commitment to Him such as walking on glass, swallowing fire or shaving your head. Nope, just be cleansed in the water. I have even known countless believers who, after rededicating themselves to the Lord, have chosen to go through the waters of baptism again as a symbol of cleansing whatever it was that had become spiritually sullied. It is a beautiful act, and the baptism services at Eastgate are among my favorite services of the year.

Next, consider that water can defeat Satan. How so? Because it is the opposite of fire, which hell is full of. Quench the fires of hell and you extinguish Satan's ultimate power. Not to mention all those pesky fiery darts (see Ephesians 6:16).

Finally, and most precious, water precedes birth. The breaking of a pregnant woman's water heralds deliverance and new life. No water, no baby.

Are you trying to birth something in your life? Then water is in your future. And in the next chapter, Chris is going to help convince you that you were born for a very specific purpose and that you have been born again for an even more spectacular one. Never water it down!

The cure for anything is salt water: sweat, tears or the sea.

Isak Dinesen, twentieth-century Danish author

4

Your Net Worth

I had someone ask me the other day, "Chris, what is your net worth?"

Without hesitation I replied, "Well, it's not a very big net, but I think I paid about $45 for it."

I'm sure that was not the answer the person was looking for, but my fisherman's sense of humor couldn't resist. And, to be gut-level honest with you, when I heard the word *net* my mind immediately went to fishing. My first thought was not my financial position. Your mind longs to go to the places where it finds the most pleasure. Yet the demands of the world may keep you from ever making it to those places.

Now, I am diligent with my finances and take seriously my stewardship of all that God brings into our household, and you should be, too! But when I think about the things that are most valuable to me, most of them cannot be measured in dollars. The things at the top of my "most valuable" list are relational, spiritual, creative, exciting and fun. Yes, I like to make money, and Laura and I have dreams on our bucket list that will require us to work

hard to generate the necessary revenue to see them come to frui-
tion. But Laura and I spend more time *spending ourselves* than
we do spending our *money*. We do what we love and love doing it!

I'm surprised how many people live their entire lives doing
things that they don't enjoy doing. Why is that? Generally, because
of two factors: fear and fear. No, that's not a typo. Fears are the
single greatest thieves of a life of purpose and pleasure. In this
chapter, I want to talk to you about your "net worth." I want to
help you discover the plans God has uniquely created for you, so
you can discover the *pleasure* that He has placed within those plans.

Let's talk about your net worth. Financially, your net worth is the
value of all of your assets minus your debts and liabilities. That might
be a positive number for you, or it might be a negative number. But
you also have a *life* net worth. It's called your *purpose*. I can assure
you that your life net worth will always be positive and growing in
Jesus. Think of it this way: Your life minus the debts and liabilities
(sin, fear, anxiety, addiction, etc.) Jesus has purchased from you will
always result in a positive and abounding life net worth. If you haven't
allowed Jesus to relieve you of those debts and liabilities, then they
will weigh heavy on your value and lower your sense of net worth.

In John chapter 10, Jesus says this: "The thief comes only to
steal and kill and destroy; I came that they may have life, and have it
abundantly" (verse 10). In Jesus, you have a value that goes beyond
your wildest imagination. Listen to this description of God from
the apostle Paul in his letter to the Ephesians: "Now to Him who
is able to do far more abundantly beyond all that we ask or think,
according to the power that works within us, to Him be the glory
in the church and in Christ Jesus to all generations forever and ever.
Amen" (Ephesians 3:20–21). Did you catch that? He is able to do
far more abundantly beyond what you can ask or think, and He is
also able to accomplish this throughout every generation of those
who believe this about Him. Your worth and value in God's eyes are
priceless and abundant through Jesus Christ. God has a plan and
purpose for your life, and that plan is so valuable that He allowed His
Son, Jesus, to come and purchase the debts and liabilities of your life
so you can be free to embrace that plan and feel His good pleasure.

How can I be so sure? Let's look at some other supporting Scriptures. You started as an original thought in God's imagination! He knew you before you were in your mother's womb (see Jeremiah 1:5). He knows the plans He has designed for your life, and they are plans that have been created to prosper you, to give you a future and a hope (see Jeremiah 29:11). You are God's masterpiece, and you were created in Christ Jesus for amazing works that God had in mind before you were even born, so that you would accomplish them (see Ephesians 2:10). When you were redeemed by salvation in Jesus, the unique gifts and talents God gave you from the very beginning became rivers of pleasure, joy and peace running through your life. They were designed not only to make your life abundant, but to spill out of you and into the lives of those around you. We will explore the different rivers of cultural impact in our society today in more detail in the chapters to come, but let me next share a little of my journey in discovering my net worth.

Natural and Acquired Gifts

I was born into a creative, entrepreneurial family. Both of my grandfathers were self-employed businessmen. Grandpa Herb Smith was a CPA by trade and an entertainer and writer at heart. My grandparents' house at 1127 Guthrie Street in Gibson City, Illinois, was an accounting firm in the basement and a music hall upstairs. A 54 Hammond B2 organ, an upright piano, an electronic rhythm machine, and a handful of Hohner mouth harps were the primary focal pieces of furniture in their living room, a room measuring no more than twelve feet by twelve feet, but tastefully done. Their house was a hub for their business and their passions.

Grandpa Ray Arnold was a jack-of-all-trades. He owned a livestock sale barn and was a builder, a glassblower and a salesman. I spent my Illinois summers as a teenager renovating rental houses he owned by day, and then we would load up the van and trailer and head to nearby county fairs for the evenings to sell handcrafted spun and blown glass trinkets and vases at the Arnold Glassblowers booth.

My father, Terry Smith, was a professional drummer who moved to Nashville, Tennessee, in the 1970s to become a recording session player. He eventually retired the drums and found there was a need in the music industry for his skills in accounting and business, which he had gained from his father. He started managing the business affairs of recording artists and worked for Roger Miller, Waylon Jennings, and the rock and roll band Dr. Hook & the Medicine Show. In the 1980s he started his own business in music publishing rights management and royalty accounting. I share these pieces of my upbringing to give light to the fact that through my family, I acquired and possess skills that are unique to me. I, too, spent twenty-plus years in the Nashville music industry. I am entrepreneurial, I am good with numbers and business, I love to design and build things, and I play guitar and write songs. I call these natural gifts and acquired gifts. The natural gifts are those tied to the DNA of my family, and the acquired gifts are the skills I learned along the way through experience and education.

Now let me add another gift into the gift mix. When I moved to Nashville from central Illinois in 1980, I thought I wanted to be an architect. But when I entered school at Belmont College (now Belmont University), I was immediately immersed in a creative culture that helped me see that my real passion was music. So I shoved my architecture dream aside and began my business degree that was specifically designed for music business. My advisor told me that if I wanted to get ahead in the music industry, I should do an internship with a record company on Nashville's famous "Music Row" while I was getting my degree. In my freshman year, I was fortunate to secure an internship with an international company called Dick James Music (DJM), which had just opened a Nashville office. DJM was the music publisher of songwriters like Neil Diamond, The Beatles, and Elton John.

The acquired gifts I gained in my three years with DJM proved foundational for my career. In 1984, I married Laura Harris and we began our incredible life together. In 1985, I was hired as general manager of the Morgan Music Group, an independent publishing company started by legendary songwriter Dennis Morgan. Dennis wrote hits for Barbara Mandrell, Charlie Pride, and Ronnie Milsap, and also huge pop hits for artists like Aretha Franklin, George Michael, Rod Stewart, and Milli Vanilli. My primary job was to sign and develop songwriters, as well as finding recording artists to record the songs the publishing company owned. Over the course of my career, the songwriters I signed or developed had their songs recorded by artists like Garth Brooks, Whitney Houston, Eric Clapton, and Amy Grant. It was during this season that I secured my first number one song as a songwriter with the song "Saved by Love," which was recorded by Amy Grant, and which I co-wrote with Amy and also Justin Peters.

I learned early on that my greatest strength was discovering and developing creative people. I have an ability to recognize potential, develop it and help it find its way. In 1992, I moved away from developing songwriters and became director of A&R (the artists and repertoire division) for Reunion Records, with the responsibility of finding and developing new Christian music artists. I had the great pleasure of discovering and developing artists like Clay Crosse, Carolyn Arends, and Michael James, and bands like Prayer Chain, Allstar United, Third Day, and Unspoken.

My natural gifts and my acquired gifts were working beautifully, and Laura and I were beginning to prosper. As my career continued to build, there was something else building inside me—my relationship with the Holy Spirit. I was fortunate to have connected with people in my business journey who had a solid and sincere faith in God. And, during this time, Laura and I had set as a priority for our marriage and family our connection to our local church. We served, we built relationships, we connected consistently and we found ourselves growing in our love for people and for God's work. We served in the nursery. We served in the children's ministry. We served in the youth department and hosted events at our home. Alongside my prospering business career, Laura and I were beginning to prosper spiritually. Suddenly, our "net worth" was increasing. God was using us to bring more and more people to Himself, and it didn't even feel like work.

Have you ever thought about your net worth? About the natural and acquired gifts that are yours because of the family you are in or the environment you grew up in? It is time for you to make a list of what those natural and acquired gifts are. In fact, we have created a helpful form for you to download so you can list these generational blessings and natural gifts that are unique to you through your family. **Download it at www.GoMakeYourSplash .com. Just click on Net Worth Form and complete page 1.**

Please notice that there is also a page 2 of that form. It provides a place for you to list your acquired gifts, such as any training you have had, college degrees or life experiences. And do you remember the equation I gave you to determine your net worth? It was:

Assets minus debts and liabilities equals net worth
(or)
Your gifts minus fears and sins equals purpose

So, next on the downloadable form is a place for you to write your fears and sins that are life patterns. This form is worth taking some time on and praying over! It helps you see what God is up to in your life, as well as what the enemy is up to. Take some time to complete these pages on your net worth before moving on. With this form completed, you will be ready to add the third component, spiritual gifts, to the mix.

Spiritual Gifts

In Jesus' famous Sermon on the Mount, He said, "Blessed [happy] are those who hunger and thirst for righteousness, for they shall be satisfied" (Matthew 5:6). In the late 1980s and early 1990s, Laura and I were hungering and thirsting for all God had in store for our lives. We knew what *we* wanted for our lives, but we were suddenly struck by this prompting to know what *God* was excited about for our lives. This was a major turning point for us. We began connecting with other hungering and thirsting believers on Friday nights for a Bible study at our home in Nashville. God used those nights to help us understand that our salvation was just the first step into His eternal and abundant life. I discovered that the Holy Spirit inside me was to be like a rushing river of pleasure, joy and peace 24/7. God's Spirit was to be the living water that Jesus spoke about to the woman at the well. We hungered and thirsted to experience the fullness of God's presence and purpose for our lives. And we found it.

In 1994, while on a business trip to Vancouver, British Columbia, I had a dramatic encounter with Jesus in my hotel room that filled me with this river of living water. I experienced what John the Baptist described that Jesus would come and do: "baptize you with the Holy Spirit and fire" (Matthew 3:11). My life, from that day until now, has been filled with spiritual purpose. I began to become keenly aware of a new set of gifts that I had not possessed before that encounter. This leads me to the third gift mix I want to add to your mix—the gifts of the Spirit. Much like my natural and acquired gifts, these newly discovered spiritual gifts were added to my life to prosper me body, mind and spirit! I felt more complete than I had ever felt before, and still do to this day.

When God adds His spiritual gifts to your natural and acquired gifts and you activate them all together, you experience the full extent of God's purpose for your life. Up to that point in time, I was prospering in my natural and acquired gifts. But when God added His Holy Spirit's gifts to those, I experienced my God-given purpose, and it changed my life forever.

You have the same mix. You have natural gifts that you received from your mother and father, and acquired gifts that you received from your experience and education. And God has made available to you spiritual gifts to be added to that mix, which will give your life everlasting purpose. To receive those gifts, you have to know Jesus not casually, but intimately. You have to become a student of God's Word. You have to serve and connect with people who are spiritually hungrier and thirstier than you! And you have to "desire earnestly spiritual gifts" (1 Corinthians 14:1). Your purpose is a beautiful, unique tapestry that weaves together when you live out these three gift mixes. There is no one else on the planet like *you*!

Yes, Purpose!

Let's go back to our net worth equations and look more closely at the second one: *Your gifts minus fears and sins equals purpose.* You might be asking, "How do fear and sin patterns take away from my purpose?" That is a great question. Because you are created in the image of your heavenly Father, your purpose is greater than you can possibly imagine, ask or think. You have tremendous potential. Imagine if others were threatened by the potential with which you were created. How would they keep you from reaching that potential? They would do everything within their ability and power to try to take it away, or even to kill you. This is why Jesus said, "The thief comes only to steal and kill and destroy" (John 10:10). There is a thief after your potential! He is a spiritual thief with an invisible army, and together they craftily wage war against your potential in God every day.

Ephesian 6:10–17 reveals who the thief and his army are, and also tells you how you can overcome their resisting forces. It has been my personal experience that the main tactics Satan and his troops use to resist my potential are fear and operating outside the will of God. Fear keeps you from moving forward into the unknown, and sin gets you off course or away from God's plan for your life.

Now imagine your life without fear, and with an ability not to get off course—or an ability to get back *on* course when you do get off course. If you have the means to remove the debts and liabilities from your assets, your net worth will increase. Jesus not only came to remove the debts and liabilities from your assets; He came to give you authority over all the power of the enemy (see Luke 10:19). This authority, given to you through Jesus and the power of the Holy Spirit, is what enables you to overcome fear. With the fear, debts and liabilities out of your way, and with the grace of the Holy Spirit empowering you, you have the ability in God to live by faith. Faith is the highway to your purpose in God.

Your unique natural, acquired and spiritual gifts have fashioned you divinely and strategically for a purpose. Your unique gift mix is designed to flow in a specific occupation or cultural river for impact.

In the coming chapters Laura and I will help you discover your cultural river(s) of impact, but let me first expound on your purpose for flowing in those rivers. It is commonly taught in the Church that disciples are to convert people to the Christian faith. I want to bring a more relational perspective to what Jesus said in Matthew 28:18–20:

> All authority has been given to Me in heaven and on earth. Go therefore and make disciples of all the nations, baptizing them in the name of the Father and the Son and the Holy Spirit, teaching them to observe all that I commanded you.

Your purpose is to "go" and to "make" disciples. *Go* is an intentional action word that means to move. So going is going to require you to move in faith, even out of your comfort zone. *Make* is a process word that means to build, construct or put together, which requires an investment of time and relationship. The purpose of making disciples requires faith and relationship. As a follower of Jesus, as a pastor and as a businessman, my purpose is not to convert people. My purpose is to introduce people to the loving, living, life-transforming Person of God through my net worth in Jesus Christ, under the power and grace of the Holy Spirit. My faith is a relationship, not a religion. Therefore, my purpose is to use all of my gift mixes, discover my river(s), and go and build relationships with people in my river(s). Then I help them find relationship with God so that they, too, can find purpose for their lives.

Your life purpose, like mine, and like that of Peter, Andrew, James and John on the Sea of Galilee, is to lower your "net" into the waters and bring a harvest of brothers and sisters into loving relationship with God and His amazing family.

What is *your* net worth? I promise you, in Jesus it is worth a whole lot more than $45!

> When the well's dry, we know the worth of water.
>
> Benjamin Franklin, American statesman,
> inventor and Founding Father

5

In over Your Head

Chris just did a fine job explaining the concept of how God has uniquely designed you with a distinct set of natural gifts (from your family) and acquired gifts (from your education and experiences). As part of this book's river theme, we are calling this concept your "net worth." I also believe this is a creative, new way to look at evangelism, seeing as how fish represent souls. Jesus has made us fishers of men!

As Chris asked at the end of the previous chapter, what was—and is—your net worth? How might God be wanting to use you in the earth in an attempt to draw all men and women to Himself? He needs you. We are all He has to work with down here!

You, therefore, need to get to know your spiritual personality very well, and we believe that in order to do that, you must first learn more about yourself. In this chapter, we are going to list and briefly define the top 20 personality tests in the world today, and then in the next chapter, Chris is going to discuss what he calls the five personalities of God. Spoiler alert: Get ready to learn a lot about yourself and God!

Personalities Are Fluid

But for starters, how did the world even first become aware of "personalities?" In the early to mid-400s BC, it was the Greek physician Hippocrates who first suggested that all human beings have a *persona*. In short, he thought that this persona was comprised of four different temperaments, and that whichever one was more prominent in a person determined his or her "humour," and therefore, unique personality. He and his later medical champion of the second century AD, Galenus, had a theory that human moods are caused by either a deficiency or excess of four main bodily fluids. Too much black bile made you "melancholic," and too much yellow-colored bile made you "choleric." Too much phlegm made you "phlegmatic," and too much blood made you "sanguine."

These physicians believed that your mood would improve as your bodily fluids were balanced. I know as a naturopathic doctor that the body and mind do greatly affect each other, but modern medicine still overlooks this. Nonetheless, the four temperaments theory (minus the bodily fluids part) has remained popular and is even used in the workplace today. It certainly was accepted in Hippocrates' day. His teachings on this spread quickly far and wide. In fact, I cannot help but wonder if they traveled by word of mouth from Greece to Israel (less than a day's boat ride away across the Mediterranean), to where Nehemiah was rebuilding the walls around Jerusalem at the same exact time. Hippocrates would have surely labeled Nehemiah a "melancholic" if he had heard his words: "'The wall of Jerusalem is broken down and its gates are burned with fire.' When I heard these words, I sat down and wept and mourned for days; and I was fasting and praying before the God of heaven" (Nehemiah 1:3–4).

Since Greece was at war with Persia three times during this century (during the years 499–449 BC), and since a Persian king was paying for Nehemiah's wall, you know that these cultures were thrown together, as were their ideologies. It sort of makes you wonder, in all the interpersonal woes that Nehemiah experienced with the Jews fighting each other during the rebuilding process, if he ever labeled their personalities with these emerging theories during the 52 days of monotonously swinging his hammer: "That sanguine thinks he's the life of this party, but he'd better get to work!" "I'm reassigning that phlegmatic from guard to builder; he won't confront the enemy!" "Who does that choleric think he is, assuming he's in charge?" And if Nehemiah was indeed diagnosing his friends' personalities with these trendsetting labels that we are still using today, he probably knew by that point that he was Mr. Melancholy.

The Inventor of Personalities

The idea of personalities sounds so common to us today, but that ancient era is where it all started. These theories found their way into all layers of society until the late 1800s, when psychologist Sigmund Freud began teaching that it was much more complex than that and needed researching. Through his teachings and suppositions, the psychodynamic approach was born. Freud basically suggested that our personality traits and our outward behavior are driven by our more hidden motives, and even by our subconscious needs. (Maybe you are familiar with his labeling of the conscious, preconscious and unconscious as the *ego*, *superego* and *id*.)

In the 1960s, Swiss psychiatrist and psychoanalyst Carl Gustav Jung insisted that there were only four main personality mechanisms: thinking, feeling, sensing and intuition (from which the Myers-Briggs Type Indicator test evolved). By the end of the twentieth century, multiple tests emerged claiming to have the true ability to identify personality. These tests especially infiltrated the workplace, helping bring clarity and definition to people who were looking to get ahead, specifically by improving their interpersonal and professional relationships, making first impressions on coworkers, gaining the emotional acceptance of others, and even increasing their productivity. Perhaps in the past, you were even hired after being asked to take a personality inventory, or you actually left a job after a taxing personality clash with another individual.

Human theories aside, if God is going to use us in our rivers of influence (and you will discover yours in part two), then we must learn what piece of *God's personality* He has invested in us (which you will discover about yourself by the end of this first part). His ideas on personality predate even all of Hippocrates' theories. That's because God invented personalities! He alone has fashioned a form of influence in you that the world needs. You will soon understand exactly why God assigned you the personality He did when He knit you in your mother's womb and then allowed you to go through all your childhood experiences. By the end of this book, you are going to love your personality. Or love it even more.

The Tests of Time

Let's take a look for a moment at how human researchers have defined you and your personality. Just as I appreciate those travel sites that show me all the various airlines at once and compare prices and times so that I don't have to make comparisons one by one, I am going to use this chapter to give you a glimpse of the top 20 popular personality tests and their most basic, defining features.

I'm most excited to tell you, however, that in chapter 9 you will be given the opportunity to take the personality test Chris and I have designed for you ourselves. It is the first ever personality test that accounts for God's personality working through yours. While every other personality test helps you assess who you *are*, we wanted to create one that also helps you become who you are *supposed to be*, based on the natural and supernatural gifts God has assigned to you. Our test is less like a snapshot and more like an ongoing movie of your life and calling. Less like a pond and more like a river. Are you ready to dive in and explore both?

First, here are those top 20 personality tests I have researched, with greater emphasis on the first eight because those are the ones I recently took myself. Perhaps you are familiar with some of these, or have taken them yourself.

- *The Big Five:* The leader in modern personality testing. The fact that other tests are more popular speaks to their aggressive marketing, but The Big Five is cited in more than 700 scientific publications and is by far the most scientifically validated psychological model. Created in the 1980s, its 120 statements that you respond to rate your traits of openness, conscientiousness, extraversion, agreeableness and neuroticism.

- *Myers-Briggs Type Indicator (MBTI):* Designed by the dynamic mother-daughter duo of Katharine Cook Briggs and Isabel Trigger Meyers in the 1940s, this test has 93 questions that label you with one of 16 personalities. The test examines four categories: introversion or extraversion, sensing or intuition, thinking or feeling, judging or perceiving. One letter from each category is taken to produce a four-letter test result such as *ISTP* or *ENFJ*.

- *Enneagram:* 108 detailed questions place you in one of nine numeric personality characteristics, labeled #1 thorough #9. Participants learn to understand how they handle stress and emotionally relate to the world around them. Because the Enneagram test offers solutions for the development of each individual type, it has become widely used by counselors, psychologists, business owners, parents and teachers. Brought to the modern world in 1915, it is thought that the Enneagram is from ancient Greek tradition since the name comes from the Greek words *ennea*, which means 9, and *gramma*, which means a written or drawn symbol.

- *The Four Temperaments Test:* Consisting of only eight questions, this helpful quiz is based on Hippocrates' theory of the four main temperaments and classifies your personality into one of four types: sanguine, phlegmatic, choleric or melancholic. These four classical temperaments are also associated with the four elements and the four seasons. Choleric temperament is associated with fire and summer. Melancholic is earth and winter. Sanguine is air and spring. Phlegmatic is autumn and water.

- *HEXACO Model of Personality Structure and Inventory:* 200 questions compiled by Canadian psychologists in the early 2000s measure human personality characteristics and define them in terms of six dimensions: Honesty-Humility (H), Emotionality (E), Extraversion (X), Agreeableness (A), Conscientiousness (C), and Openness to Experience (O). These factors tend to be uncorrelated with each other. That is, high levels of one trait do not necessarily suggest high or low levels of another.

- *Workplace DISC:* The DISC model of behavior was introduced in 1928 by physiological psychologist William Moulton Marston. The Workplace DISC is a series of 28 questions that help determine your levels of dominance, influence, steadiness and conscientiousness. It is used by more than one million people every year to help enhance workplace teamwork, productivity and communication.

- *True Colors:* In 1978, Don Lowry, a student of the Keirsey Temperament Sorter (which we will highlight in a moment), developed this system, which uses four primary colors to designate personalities and behavioral styles. One of four colors—green, orange, gold and blue—is assigned based on four basic learning styles: pragmatic planners, independent thinkers, people-oriented types and action-oriented types. This test was actually created to categorize at-risk youth and help identify their strengths.

- *Rorschach Inkblot Test:* Definitely one of the most eccentric and amusing personality assessments out there, this one is done in person. An examiner shows the participant an inkblot and then asks the person to describe what he or she sees. Answers reveal the psychological state in participants as young as age five.

- *High5 Test:* This test involves completing 100 questions in 20 minutes that are designed to discover your natural strengths.
- *Minnesota Multiphasic Personality Inventory (MMPI):* This test has 567 true-or-false questions that are useful in observing adult psychopathology and personality. It is often used to diagnose mental illness.
- *The 16 Personality Factor Questionnaire (16PF):* This test involves 30 minutes of testing that measure your perfectionism, warmth, sensitivity, boldness, etc.
- *Revised NEO Personality Inventory:* This test consists of 240 items and takes 30–40 minutes to complete. It is based on the same 5 personality attributes studied in the Big Five and the HEXACO models.
- *Eysenck Personality Inventory:* These 100 questions measure two distinct dimensions of personality: introverts versus extraverts, and stability versus neuroticism.
- *The Caliper Profile:* This test involves job-based skill assessments that help discover employees' true motives and help with job placement and productivity. You will need two hours to answer these 180 multiple-choice questions.
- *The Birkman Method:* These 298 questions (mostly true or false) and 32 scales mostly measure occupational assessment, talents, social behaviors and, of course, personality.
- *Values and Motives Inventory (VMI):* This requires 20 minutes' worth of testing on your intrinsic, extrinsic and interpersonal motives and evaluates where you are most likely to gain occupational satisfaction.
- *Personality Assessment Inventory (PAI):* These 344 questions examine psychopathological and personality traits across four scales: clinical skills, treatment consideration skills, interpersonal skills and validity scales.

- *Californian Psychological Inventory (CPI):* For anyone over the age of 13, this inventory contains 434 true-or-false questions and analyzes everyday behavior across 18 scales.
- *Keirsey Temperament Sorter:* This theory expounds on Hippocrates' temperament research (as does the Four Temperaments Test), categorizing personalities as artisans, idealists, rationals or guardians. These personalities are then each divided into two categories that also have two role variants, for a total of 16 personality types that correlate with the Myers-Briggs Type Indicator.
- *Color Code Personality Assessment:* This test claims not only to help identify what you do, but also why you do it. It is a free test that places you in one of four color categories: whites, reds, yellows and blues.

Regarding children's tests, *National Geographic* also has personality quizzes for children in which kids can find out which type of forest animal, mythical creature, dinosaur or Egyptian pharaoh they are most like. They can also take a quiz that tells them which time period they really should have been born in. The opening words to that quiz are, "Were you born a couple hundred years too late? Or a thousand years too early?" Hmmm. It is all for fun, but Chris and I feel we should be planting destiny, not doubt, within our children. And within you.

Allow Me

Let me now use myself as an example of how consistently these tests can score you. Then afterward, I will tell you where they fall short. I took the time to test myself with almost half of these (the first eight tests I listed, which took about four hours), and here is how I scored:

The Big Five: I scored 100 percent in extraversion (how outgoing and social a person is).

Myers-Briggs Type Indicator (MBTI): I scored as an *ENFJ* (Extraverted, iNtuitive, Feeling, Judging); I am "the teacher."

HEXACO Model: I scored highest in extraversion (which this test defines as social boldness and liveliness). I scored second highest in conscientiousness (organization and diligence).

Enneagram: I scored as a #1: "the moral perfectionist and reformer." We #1 types press to know the rules/boundaries, and then we follow them and defend them to others.

The Four Temperaments: I scored as choleric first (brave, ambitious and fiery), and sanguine second (creative, goal-oriented, optimistic).

Workplace DISC: I scored highest in "dominance."

True Colors: I scored as gold, a detailed and responsible type. A gold loves following rules—after asking lots of questions so they become clearer—and gets frustrated with those who don't follow them.

Rorschach Inkblot Test: After staring at ten pictures for patterns (and not liking any of the multiple choice options), I tested "95 percent absolutely normal." I was immediately bothered by what unnamed 5 percent of me was "abnormal," so I retook the test three more times, trying to get a perfect score . . . which should tell you everything you need to know about me. The score got lower and lower every time I retested, until I finally took a deep breath, snapped out of my driven daze, and realized that you would rather have my honesty than my perfection. *This* is the plight of a #1, extravert, choleric, dominant, moral perfectionist reformer. A 95 percent is not good enough. And *not* because you are insecure, prideful or competitive. You just think the world deserves 100 percent out of you and 100 percent out of *everyone* if it is going to become a better place. And you are just optimistic enough to believe it can happen. That is a day in the life of my head!

Based on the analytics of some of my testing, only 3 percent of the world is like me, which means (due to my social boldness) that I spend a great deal of time trying to convince the other 97 percent why they should consider my ideas. Not because I feel superior to them (or inferior if they won't listen), but because I instinctively work hard to come up with the solution that is good for the whole team, and then I genuinely hope that it will be trusted. If you ever hear me say the words "I trust you in this," and I then defer to your wisdom, that is the highest compliment I can pay you.

No Comparison

To summarize, the secular world is full of personality inventories that will tell you everything you ever (or never) wanted to know about yourself. But if you are not careful, you will be in over your head with information overload. And while these tests are scarily accurate about your persona and motives, none of them tell you how you relate to the world spiritually—especially in secular places—and how you can most naturally exhibit God's personality to those around you based on His tailor-made calling for your life. Remember, the upcoming test Chris and I have designed for you is less of a snapshot and more like an ongoing movie of your life and calling. Less like a pond and more like a river!

Finally, please notice that all those other tests compare you to others and lump you into categories with people just like you. But the test you are about to take in chapter 9 compares you to your heavenly Father alone. He is the one you want to look like! Some of His traits stand out to others immediately about you, just as someone might say you have your earthly father's eyes or your mother's mouth. And there are other traits of God that you may have to mature into. If you have never considered the fact that God has a personality, it is time to do so. And it is time to learn which piece of His personality you mirror to the world.

> In order to reflect, think and plan, you must quiet yourself. You can't see your reflection in churning waters. Water must be still to see your reflection.
>
> Karen Susman, American tennis player
> and Wimbledon Champion

6

Born of Water and Spirit

Laura just told you that she is optimistic, but she also says that I am "optimistic . . . to a fault" (which actually makes her the realist in our relationship). I am definitely a glass-half-full kind of guy. I get this from my mother, Jackie Curtis, and she got this from her mother, my Grandma Dorty. When Laura finished her doctorate in naturopathy, we had a party, and she received all kinds of gifts she could use as a naturopath. One of those items was a blood type test kit. She was so excited about the test kit that she used me as her guinea pig. Interestingly and thankfully, my health has been so good through all my years that I didn't even know my blood type. I jokingly told her before taking the test, "Surely I'm a B+, because I'm a pretty positive guy!"

Laura rolled her eyes, but much to her surprise, the results of the test confirmed it. I am a B+ guy through and through. It's not only one of my personality traits; it runs in my veins! Thank you, Mom!

In the previous chapter, Laura explained some of the most popular personality tests used today. But did you know that long before society had personality tests, Scripture revealed that God has a personality? In fact, Scripture shows that God can manifest His personality in one of five ways through you. In this chapter, I am going to explain what that looks like. And in the next, Laura is going to compare those five personalities of God to five bodies of water, so that when you discover what your spiritual personality type is, you will know how to flow into your river and what your role will be in that industry. The good news is that by the time you finish part one, you will know which spiritual personality type you possess. (It may even be more than one.) We have created a platform where you can take an interactive test and not have to calculate your own scores. Everything will be done for you right there.

But first, think of this: When you came into this world you were born of water, and you brought with you all the genetic traits of your earthly family—some good and some not so good! As we discussed in chapter 4, you were born with generational blessings from your family line that define the unique mix of natural gifts you possess. Add to that all your acquired gifts, training and experiences, and you are one of a kind.

Along with all these gifts, you also inherited a circuitry of emotional and psychological responses that further make you even more intricately unique. Whereas your natural and acquired gifts are expressed through your physical body, your personality is expressed through your soul: your mind, will and emotions.

Most of my personality traits appear to stem more from my mother's side of the family. I am positive. I like to laugh. I prefer to be lighthearted, as opposed to serious, but I can be serious when necessary. I am a thinker. A man of fewer words, preferring sentences over paragraphs. I tend to be more merciful than judgmental. In my mom, I can see clear genetic similarities. So much so that when Laura thinks my positivity is being a little too optimistic and minimizing a hurdle just in front of us, she'll say "Okay, Jackie!"

Most people live their lives entirely on the basis of their natural and acquired gifts and the feelings inside their soul (again, the mind, will and emotions). They live and die having never experienced anything more than what they were handed biologically and environmentally. Think for a minute about the life you were handed. Maybe you came from a solid family with very little hardship or emotional challenges. Or maybe you experienced the opposite and have been handed a life of pain and suffering, and you have asked God, *Why me?* God didn't hand you these generational debts and liabilities, however. They were handed to you through the generational sin in your family history. The Scriptures discuss visiting the sins of the fathers on the children for many generations (see Exodus 34:6–8). Many people refer to these as generational curses.

But there is good news! These spiritual generational traits don't have to be part of your future. Many people are familiar with the term "born again" as it relates to the Christian faith, but an astounding number of people don't understand that this term means a literal second birth. The second birth refers to being born again of the Spirit of God. You are born again of the Spirit when you receive Jesus Christ as your Savior and Lord. In fact, Jesus explained to Nicodemus that it is essential to be born again of the Spirit in order to *see* and *enter* the Kingdom of God (see John 3:3–5).

Jesus goes on to say that "that which is born of the flesh [water] is flesh, and that which is born of the Spirit is spirit" (John 3:6). Being born again of the Spirit is not a religious term; it is an actual life transformation that results in your becoming a new creation. It is the process of having the debts and liabilities stripped from your net worth, and having an investment of heavenly proportions added to your net worth, making your life worth living. This heavenly investment is the person and persona of God living inside you.

When you are born again of the Spirit, you carry within you both the gifts and the personality of your heavenly Father. I know you have been born of water if you are reading this, but have you been born again of the Spirit? If not, stop right here and pray the ABC's of being born again of the Spirit. (A) Acknowledge your need for God's love. (B) Believe that Jesus came to take away all your debts and liabilities. (C) Confess Jesus as the supreme authority over your future (no worldly compromises). And I'll add (D) *Deliver to me, Father, Your Holy Spirit so that I can be born again of the Spirit.*

If you will pray this with a sincere and contrite heart and will commit to allow God to live through you, then you will be on your way to a brand-new life!

Consecrated and Appointed

Did you know that your spiritual personality began forming before you were ever even in your mother's womb? In chapter 4, I mentioned a passage out of Jeremiah 1, where God said He knew the prophet before he was in his mother's womb. In verse 5 God tells him, "Before I formed you in the womb I knew you, and before you were born I consecrated you; I have appointed you a prophet to the nations." We see that before Jeremiah was formed in his mother's womb, God knew him, *consecrated* him and *appointed* him for a unique purpose, to be a prophet to the nations. The same process is true for you. You were *consecrated* and *appointed* by God before your conception.

Let's look at those two words *consecrated* and *appointed* for a minute. *Consecrated* in the original Hebrew translation is the word *qadas* (pronounced kaw-DASH'), and it means "be set apart or to be holy, pure, dedicated or prepared by God."[1] God's plans for you from before the beginning were for you to be holy, pure, dedicated or prepared by and for Him. Secondly, you were *appointed*, which in Hebrew is the word *natan* (pronounced naw-THAN'), meaning "to be bestowed with, employed, or to be granted or made to be."[2]

When you combine these two concepts, you can see that God has *bestowed upon* you a purpose that is *holy* to Him, and that you were set apart for Him before you were born. Paul supports this idea in his letter to the Ephesians when he writes, "For we are His workmanship, created in Christ Jesus for good works, which God prepared beforehand so that we would walk in them" (Ephesians 2:10). The Spirit of God has been placed inside you so that you carry the attributes of your heavenly Father with you wherever you go. These attributes were consecrated and appointed by God, given to you through Jesus, and now live inside you in the person of the Holy Spirit.

The Five Personalities of God

What is this new, consecrated and appointed life supposed to look like in you? Does God strip away all your natural gifts, acquired gifts and personality and replace those with something new? Absolutely not. When you are born of the Spirit, you will still have your natural and acquired gifts and talents, but you will also be given spiritual gifts and a piece (or pieces) of your Father's personality. In his letter to the church of Ephesus, Paul describes five personality types that God would give to the Church to equip the saints and build the Body of Christ: "And He gave some as apostles, some as prophets, some as evangelists, some as pastors and teachers, for the equipping of the saints for the work of ministry, for the building up of the body of Christ" (Ephesians 4:11–12 NASB2020).

In some churches, those five "labels" are referred to as the *fivefold ministry* of the Church, or the *offices* of the Church. But Laura and I hope to bring a more personal understanding to these five attributes of God, so that you can embrace them and apply them to your life, for God's intended purpose. I am therefore going to refer to them as the *five personality types* of God, for the sake of our conversation in this book.

Laura and I both believe in and celebrate the fivefold offices of apostle, prophet, evangelist, pastor and teacher in the Church. We understand that referring to them as five personality types might bring a new perspective to you, but we believe you will see what a huge blessing it is to receive not just an office, but pieces of your Father's personality. Each personality type we will look at comes with a distinct attribute that gives us a glimpse of the Father. You were created in His image, and when you receive pieces of His personality, you receive a new and dynamic means through which to make Him known in the earth. Laura and I want all of God's children to discover their Father's multifaceted personality so He can add Himself to them in such a way that the world sees their good deeds and glorifies Him. Let's look more closely at these five personality types of God revealed to us in Scripture.

The Apostle

You know who the apostles were in the New Testament, but what do apostles do? Simply stated, an apostle is one who commissions, encourages and inspires others. They are like good fathers, like God is a good Father. Jesus looked to His Father for direction, confidence, identity and power. Jesus' identity was established in

His Father because of the way in which God led Him and sent Him. Remember, "sent one" is what *apostle* means.

Jesus even said, "Truly, truly, I say to you, the Son can do nothing of Himself, unless it is something He sees the Father doing; for whatever the Father does, these things the Son also does in like manner" (John 5:19). The loving leadership of fatherhood is the simplest way to define the activity of an apostle. The most important attributes of an apostolic personality are love, trustworthiness and faithfulness. With this persona, the apostolic personality has the ability to inspire others into their life purpose.

The Prophet

The prophetic activity of God is often misunderstood because this attribute of His persona enables you to hear, see and understand things that others cannot. A prophetic person discerns and understands the hidden things of God. The Father, Son and Holy Spirit have the ability to simultaneously see the beginning and the end of time, and they grace your physical senses to be able to participate in what they want to reveal.

Embracing the prophetic activity of God requires tremendous faith, but also requires tremendous humility. Be careful! Your ability to accurately convey the heart, personality and will of God through this grace is subjected to your physical nature. If the body and soul are not in subjection to the Holy Spirit, the information received will be tainted.

The pure prophetic personality of God, however, will be graced by, and will exhibit the fruit of the Spirit of God (see Galatians 5:22–23). When Jesus operated in the prophetic, He changed people's lives and inspired them into relationship with the Father.

The Evangelist

The evangelistic personality of God draws people to Himself. An evangelist is often described as a preacher or one who heralds Good News. Evangelistic activities are responsible for bringing people back into fellowship with their heavenly Father. With an emphasis on the Good News, this personality type in God brings hope, peace and joy to a world that is lost in hopelessness, fear and desperation.

Embracing the evangelistic heart of God enables you to speak confidently to people, either one-on-one, in group settings or even at large events, about your faith in God, the works of Jesus and the abilities of the Holy Spirit. You must have a clear understanding of the Kingdom of God and eternal life to accurately represent the heart of God as an effective evangelist. Oftentimes, evangelists will resort to fear, judgment and condemnation to reflect God's will through their evangelistic activities, but Jesus used an uncompromising, yet loving conveyance of the truth to draw crowds of thousands into repentance and healing. Speaking the truth in love is a key characteristic of the evangelistic heart of God.

The Pastor

The pastor represents the caring and nurturing personality of God. Jesus was described as the Good Shepherd. A shepherd in biblical times cared for, protected and spent long days and even nights with the sheep to ensure their survival and well-being. The pastoral heart of God is most commonly demonstrated through serving.

Jesus Himself told His disciples that He had not come to be served, but to serve (see Matthew 20:25–28). God displayed this to the Israelites in their years of wandering through the desert. He protected, provided, served and led them patiently to their Promised Land.

Carrying the pastoral personality of God, you will exhibit His faithfulness, His nurturing, His care for people in both the hardest seasons of their lives, as well as in the victories of their lives. You will do this with or without thanks and praise, because you know that it is ultimately God who gets the glory as you roll your sleeves up and serve with a smile on your face.

The Teacher

It is at the core of God's heart to teach, because again, He is a Father who wants good things for His children. To exhibit the heart of God as a teacher, you must identify more with the activity than with the art of being a teacher. A teacher gives instructions on how to learn and accomplish things through practical measures.

God used everyday life circumstances to instruct Israel throughout its history. Jesus used parables to convey truths so people could understand them and make application of those truths to their lives. The goal of a teacher with God's personality is not to gain the title of theologian. God teaches to keep His people on track with Him, and you are to do the same.

There are a great many models and methods for learning. Seminaries, hermeneutics, debate, theological discourse—all are good for reasoning out the truth. Yet instructors with a heart after God will focus less on the art and models of theological methodologies, and more on personal application of truth. True teachers are not motivated to teach *what* they know, but rather *Whom* they know. As a teacher personality, you will enjoy sharing your personal experiences through mentorship, writing and relationships built on the love you have for others and the value you place on them.

God's Personas Plus Your Humanity

Now you know the five personality types of God. And now you can see why we consider them to be more than offices. Offices are for some, but resembling our Father is for all.

These are temperaments. Traits. Characteristics. Attributes. And yes, each one—the apostle, the prophet, the evangelist, the pastor, the teacher—will come with its own peculiar and beautiful idiosyncrasies when manifested through your humanity.

In the next chapter, Laura will explore that idea with you at length. And this B+ type guy is positive that you will enjoy it.

Water is always working, reorganizing the land.

Tim Palmer, American photographer, and author of
31 books on rivers, conservation and adventure travel

7

Uncharted Waters

I love the Tim Palmer quote that Chris ended his previous chapter with about how water is always working and reorganizing the land. But have you ever wondered how a river starts? You know where many of them end—in an ocean—but have you ever given any thought to where they start? The answer is, up in the clouds. Do you remember in chapter 1 when I explained how I stayed up all night preparing the first teaching on this rivers of influence concept? I mentioned how in the wee hours of that morning, I had taken the time to create a 30-minute video to play during my teaching that contained images and stock video of this very thing . . . a drop of water's journey from the clouds in the sky to forming the rivers below. That video is not posted anywhere online, but recently, while watching one of my favorite movies, I noticed a scene where the director had already created another one for me. I have seen this movie dozens of times over the decades—maybe close to two hundred times since we own it—and perhaps you have seen it, too: *The Sound of Music.*

Whether or not you have seen it before, I ask you at least to go watch the opening scene. Turn the volume up as high as you can and notice for the first 56 seconds that there is no music—just the sounds of nature, particularly the wind. The first thing you will see is clouds, followed by skies, then mountaintops with snow. At 00:57 seconds you see greenery for the first time, and at 1:01 you see the first river down below, off to the right. Director of photography Ted McCord did a tremendous job capturing all of this from a helicopter, no doubt under the supervision of director Robert Wise. Birds finally chirp at 1:03, you hear the first music at 1:16, and then at 2:18 you finally see a little spec on the screen that, with zooming cameras, becomes Julie Andrews. Finally, at 2:41 she spins and belts out, "The hills are alive with the sound of music!"

I once read an interview with Julie Andrews in which she described how this shot was tremendously difficult to get because it was filmed on a rainy day on the top of this German mountain. They waited hours for the sun before it finally peeked out for twenty minutes, during which time the helicopter made nine attempts to swoop in and get her spinning shot. The propellers spit water and debris, mussed her hair and soiled her clothes each time, demanding a fast wardrobe change between the nine takes. Now, that's determination.

But if you will rewind to the very beginning of the film and watch it again, you will witness an even greater example of determination as you see how one drop of water in a cloud journeys to become a raging river. So now you know where rivers begin, in the heavens. Cumulonimbus (rain) clouds create snow-topped mountains. The snow melts and then trickles down over craggy rocks to become babbling brooks, which then empty into quiet streams that eventually flow downstream until they converge and become a rushing river. The same journey happens in warmer climates, too. Just faster.

Even though I planned weeks ago to share this example with you from the opening scene of *The Sound of Music*, as providence would have it, I am actually writing this book now from the Trapp Family Lodge in Stowe, Vermont, owned and operated by the von Trapps. They are, of course, the family whose harrowing World War II musical story is what the film is based on.

Chris and I were planning a getaway for our 38th anniversary—which also included time to work on this book, in addition to filming some episodes of my television show, *theTHREE*—and Vermont was one of our stops. But we had not yet secured the lodging we really wanted. Then, a few weeks ago, while watching the movie to chart the timestamps for you that I just referenced, it suddenly crossed my mind to do a web search on whether or not there were any von Trapp children still alive. Lo and behold, there are! And they are running a family lodge in Vermont!

We quickly booked a room, and wouldn't you know it, we arrived at the lodge on the very day I was to be writing this chapter using *The Sound of Music* opening scene as a visual aid for you. You can even to go theTHREE.tv to see the episodes we shot with the von Trapps while at their lodge, including an interview with the actress who played little Gretl in the film, Kym Karath. And again, I urge you to watch the opening scene from the movie itself and see exactly what I am describing to you about how rivers are born in the heavens.

But what is even more miraculous than rivers being born in the heavens is how personalities are also born in the heavens—actually *in* heaven—where your Father lives and oversees the miraculous moment of creation for each of us. Did you know that He oversaw yours? And He carefully chose for you a special piece of His personality to show to the world, long before you ever arrived earthside.

In the previous chapter, Chris ended by highlighting where God's five personalities are first introduced to us in Scripture (see Ephesians 4). And in the next chapter, he is going to blow you away with examples of how Jesus moved in each one of His Father's five personalities. Chris will also give you Scriptures for each temperament so you can see how each interacts with the others. And here, although we have been discussing the charted course of a drop of rain, I titled this chapter "*Uncharted* Waters" because I am introducing to you a concept that has never been presented:

comparing the five personalities of God (the fivefold ministry) to individual bodies of water so you can remember how those personalities flow in the earth today.

Many Christians refer to these five labels—apostles, prophets, evangelists, pastors, teachers—as offices. But they are not just for ordained people who have been to seminary or who lead a mega-church or have a television ministry. They are for the marketplace. For your workplace. For your neighborhood. And for your family table. In this chapter, you will learn about those comparisons of God's personalities to different bodies of water, so that as you learn how those waters flow into rivers, you can also discover how *you* are to flow throughout this earth into your river(s). Remember what God told me on the night that this concept was first given to me: *Mountains don't move, but rivers flow everywhere and touch everything.*

In short, let's continue to celebrate the fivefold ministry offices and give honor to those who hold them, while merely adding to this the understanding that the giftings that come with them are not for a chosen few in ministry. They are for everyone. They are for you! If you can deepen your friendship with God, and really explore these temperaments and mirror His personality traits in your day-to-day life at home and work, then you have a greater chance of being used by God both inside *and* outside church walls. Remember, there are 168 hours in each week. You are only in a church building for 2 of them!

As we now launch into discovering how each of these five personalities flows through culture, let's first define each one, along with identifying its symbolic body of water. You will learn a lot about yourself as we define these. I rarely quote Wikipedia in my published works, but for concrete geographical definitions it cannot be matched for thoroughness with brevity. Let's start with *river*: "a natural flowing watercourse, usually freshwater, flowing towards an ocean, sea, lake or another river."[1]

Picture your favorite river you have ever stood by. If you don't have a favorite, google "river videos" and find one. With that picture in mind, you are now ready to imagine these symbolic bodies of water merging into it. We are going to deviate a bit here from the Ephesians 4 order and begin with *pastors* since we are certain that this will be the one role most familiar to everyone across denominational lines.

The Pastor Personality: Society's Gentle Streams

"A stream is a continuous body of surface water flowing within the bed and banks of a channel."[2]

I believe all pastor personalities are like gentle streams, meaning that they have a gentle, peaceful effect on people. They may have personas that are larger than life and they may even shout from the pulpit (if they have one), but a true "pastor" will calm you down along your life journey, not rough you up. You may or may not be an actual, full-time pastor, but if you have a pastoral personality, then you are the friend whom someone calls when he or she is hurting. Yours is the office at work that others step into, shut the door and confess their fears and faults in.

Just as streams are narrow, someone with a pastoral heart and temperament will have the reputation of walking "the straight and narrow" path. If that's you, you are a good friend to have in a valley. You know the way out. And you not only flow from place to place with predictability, but others also come to you to find refreshment. Picture someone kneeling down by a gentle stream, cupping his hands, running them through the water and then up to his mouth to quench his thirst. *That* is how people feel after being around you. You are not designed for people to dive into. You are not over their heads. But you are consistent and transparent, and you never run dry with encouragement for others.

A pure pastor personality has a compassionate perspective and tells others,

"Don't be so hard on yourself. Try again tomorrow."
"I'm sad when you're sad. How can I help right here, right now?"
"You did it! I'm so proud of you. Let's celebrate!"
"Stay the course. God sees your heart. So do I."

If you find yourself making this type of compassionate affirmation often, you likely have a pastoral personality. If you say these things sometimes but not always, it could be that you are a hybrid between two or more of the five personalities. Let's take a look at another one and you will see what I mean.

The Prophet Personality: Underground Waterways

"A subterranean river is a river [underground waterway] that runs wholly or partly beneath the ground surface—one where the riverbed does not represent the surface of the Earth. . . . [They] may be entirely natural, flowing through cave systems."[3]

If you have a prophetic personality, then you are deep and you never run dry of revelation and advice for others. You sometimes feel hidden, not seen or appreciated by enough people. But other times, you actually hide yourself, and as the underground waterway is described above, you may flow naturally in and out of many caves (seasons of solitude).

You are a loyal friend, but your friends don't come to you to feel sunshine on their faces. They come to you for truth and insight. Your depth of insight is matched only by your depth in prayer. You comprehend its power, and you wish you could hide yourself more in it. Just as every underground river eventually comes up to the surface and sees the sun, however, you do "come up for air" and long to share with others what you have learned and heard while in prayer.

You are direct, and clear. What people see is what they get, and how you flow at lower altitudes and higher ones is the same. Just as there is over a thousand times more water underground than we see above ground in all the world's rivers and lakes, even when you are up and out, there is still more to you than meets the eye. You are always bursting at the seams with revelation, and you don't like to be contained. Any prophetic personality who longs to live on the riverbanks, constantly releasing their revelation, and who doesn't enjoy going low and flowing deeply, as they were created to do, most certainly is an amalgamation with another personality type such as the teacher personality.

A pure prophetic personality has a corrective perspective and tells others,

> "Haven't you been around this mountain before? Do you maybe see a pattern in your life?"
> "I saw this coming. I had a feeling, but don't worry . . . I've been praying for you."
> "We will fast and pray, and I'm certain that God will show us the solution."
> "You stayed the course. I knew you would! I see success written all over you."

The Teacher Personality: Tributaries

"A tributary, or affluent, is a stream or river that flows into a larger stream or main stem (or parent) river or a lake. A tributary does not flow directly into a sea or ocean."[4] For example, the Illinois River is a tributary of the Mississippi River.

If you have never seen a tributary, stop right now and go do a web search using the words *aerial view of river tributaries*. Now scroll. Do you see all those little twists and turns of life-bearing waterways? That's what the teacher personality looks like. One minute you think you are talking about something simple, and the next thing you know, this teacher-type person changes course in midstream and goes off on a tangent that, if you pay close enough attention, will actually solve your problem.

If you are a teacher personality, you always have at least two sermons or life lessons in your head that could help someone. Parables and illustrations flow from you like melted butter. A pure teacher personality has an instructional perspective and tells others,

> "First of all . . ."
> "You could have done better, true. What did you learn?"
> "I know exactly how you feel. Let me give you a game-changing solution that worked for me."
> "You are a shining example of 'what to do.' May I call on you to share with others so that they can avoid potential pitfalls, too?"

The Evangelist Personality: Whitewater Rapids

"Whitewater forms in a rapid context, in particular, when a river's gradient changes enough to generate so much turbulence that air is trapped within the water. This forms an unstable current that froths, making the water appear opaque and white."[5]

Have you ever watched a movie scene of a rescue from the fierceness of whitewater rapids? Like maybe from the movie *The River Wild* (1994, with Meryl Streep and Kevin Bacon)? Someone is saved from impending danger and a sure death on the raging river by someone else who is willing to put himself or herself in harm's way. If you have ever watched a scene like that in any film or documentary, then you have seen the heart of the evangelist personality. Whitewater rapids are classified for the purposes of boater safety, ranging from class 1 (the easiest and safest) to class 6 (the most difficult and dangerous). Experts disagree on whether or not there should actually be a class 6, since these waters are totally impassable and cannot be traversed. So for the purpose of our analogy, we will focus on class 5 here, which is characterized by extremely difficult, long and very violent rapids with highly congested routes that should be scouted from shore. Rescue conditions are difficult, and there is a significant hazard to life in the event of a mishap.

I am going to compare the evangelist personality to people who not only live with the class 5 mindset, but *they are* the class 5 whitewater rapids. They rescue others who are on their way to a sure eternal death, but after snatching them away, they place them in another current that is just as fast—now flowing upstream— toward eternal life.

The evangelist personality sees the entire world through the lens of eternity. If that's you, then you look at people as either lost or saved, whereas the teacher personality sees them as good or bad and the prophet sees them as right or wrong. A pure evangelist personality has an eternal perspective and tells others,

"Life is too short for hobbies. We must be about the work of the ministry."

"What can man do to you, friend? Be brave and courageous."
"I don't ever want to retire. I want it said of me when I die that I left it all on the field."
"If you fell asleep and died tonight, where would you wake up?"

The Apostle Personality: Estuaries

The description of an estuary is a little longer than the others:

An estuary is a partially enclosed coastal body of brackish water with one or more rivers or streams flowing into it, and with a free connection to the open sea. Estuaries form a transition zone between river environments and maritime environments. . . . Estuaries are subject both to marine influences such as tides, waves, and the influx of saline water, and to fluvial influences such as flows of freshwater and sediment. The mixing of seawater and freshwater provides high levels of nutrients both in the water column and in sediment, making estuaries among the most productive natural habitats in the world.[6]

If a drop of water is the beginning of a river, then the estuary is its end. It is where the stream meets the tide. Where fresh water and saltwater mix. It is where rivers retire and are reinvented as oceans. Likewise, the apostolic personality is the person in the conversation who brings everyone together. He or she prioritizes order and unity.

If you are an apostolic personality, you are a natural when it comes to seeing a problem and getting it solved. You set goals and work toward them. A pure apostle personality has a big-picture perspective and tells others,

"Don't just pray for *your* church. Pray for *all* the churches in your city."
"This could be streamlined a lot better so that more people can partake. I have an idea."
"I'm proud of you. Thank you for being a team player."
"So, here's what we're going to do . . ."

Do you ever catch yourself saying any of these things? Maybe in one or two categories? Listening to yourself speak is the first clue as to what your spiritual personality is, since "the mouth speaks out of that which fills the heart" (Matthew 12:34).

Highlighting Jesus

In the next chapter, you are in for a treat. You are going to get to listen to Jesus' own words as *He* shows us what a pastor personality sounds like, what a prophet personality sounds like, and so on. Chris has prepared an exhaustive biblical list of references for you so you can see exactly what each personality type looked like on Jesus in His various encounters with others. He perfectly personified the five personalities of God while on earth. And He still does!

Chapter by chapter in this first part of the book, you are inching closer to discovering exactly what your spiritual personality is. Then of course in the next part, you will learn all about your river of influence, and how your personality can make a splash there.

> Some Christians sail their boat in such low spiritual waters that the keel scrapes on the gravel all the way to Heaven, instead of being carried on a floodtide.
>
> Charles Spurgeon, influential English theologian of the 1800s
> also known as the "Prince of Preachers"

8

Go with the Flow

Being the father of six children and, at the time of this writing, the grandfather of fourteen, I have had the beautiful honor of getting to watch them grow into some of the most extraordinary people I know. Yesterday, while in Newport, Rhode Island, writing this manuscript, Laura and I received a text from our daughter Jeorgi. The text message was a video clip of her encouraging her seven-month-old son, Arlo, to say *mama*. The look on Arlo's face was priceless. His eyes were as wide open as they could possibly be, his feet and legs were kicking in the air, and he was desperately trying to form the syllables Jeorgi was demonstrating for him over and over again. With a few sporadic bursts of sound from Arlo that somewhat resembled the word *mama*, Jeorgi's excitement and loving encouragement nearly brought me to tears. Her patience, love and devotion to this next step in Arlo's growth was profoundly beautiful.

I know many of you have experienced this very same moment. You are still growing too, spiritually, and I hope you have faith that the Father is cheering you on to receive all He has planned for you. As Laura described in the previous chapter, God wants to encourage you to learn how to express His personalities through your life. We have already discussed what these five personality types are, and in this chapter I want to take you on a journey through Scripture to see how Jesus displayed His Father's personality traits everywhere He went.

What I am about to show you in the Bible revolutionized how I interact with people through the beautiful attributes of God's personality in me. Are you ready for God to express Himself through you in a new way? Let me show you what I discovered. In the spring of 2017, I sensed the Spirit of God saying to me in an inaudible voice, *Read through the gospels and notice how often Jesus' actions were apostolic, prophetic, evangelistic, pastoral, or educational as a teacher . . .*

I had never considered this before. I purchased five different colored highlighters—blue, red, yellow, orange and green. Whenever Jesus acted apostolically, I highlighted the verse in blue. When He spoke prophetically, I highlighted the verse in red. I highlighted in yellow those passages that revealed Him moving evangelistically. Orange was for when He was pastoral. And green was for when He instructed as a teacher. As we established before, these five labels are found in Ephesians 4:11–13 (NASB2020):

> And He gave some as apostles, some as prophets, some as evangelists, some as pastors and teachers, for the equipping of the saints for the work of ministry, for the building up of the body of Christ; until we all attain to the unity of the faith, and of the knowledge of the Son of God, to a mature man, to the measure of the stature which belongs to the fullness of Christ.

With my five highlighters, I read each familiar story with fresh eyes and ears, and with great anticipation. What I immediately began to notice was how naturally Jesus flowed in and out of these different attributes of His Father, and how gracefully and effectively each trait enriched, charged or even challenged the person or persons whom He encountered. It was here that I first began to realize that these five "offices" were more than offices. They were the multifaceted expressions of God's personality being manifested through Jesus' ministry.

Jesus said, "Truly, truly, I say to you, the Son can do nothing of Himself, unless it is something He sees the Father doing; for whatever the Father does, these things the Son also does in like manner" (John 5:19). The phrase "in like manner" means "in the same way." Jesus expressed Himself in the same way as His Father. His ways were apostolic, prophetic, evangelistic, pastoral, and educational as a teacher. Let me define these five personality types using key phrases described in their original Greek form:

> *Apostle*—Greek *apostolos*, meaning sent, to send, called, to call, commissioned, to commission, appoint, command. This is the big-picture perspective.
>
> *Prophet*—Greek *prophētēs*, meaning know, perceive, foretell, discern, speak, make known, warn. This is the corrective perspective.
>
> *Evangelist*—Greek *euangelistēs*, meaning to herald, to draw, to preach salvation. This is the eternal perspective.
>
> *Pastor*—Greek *poimēn*, meaning care, manage, direct, oversee, protect, encourage. This is the compassionate perspective.
>
> *Teacher*—Greek *didaskalos*, meaning teach, instruct. This is the instructional perspective.[1]

As I began to read and highlight the gospels, I was amazed at how fluidly Jesus flowed in and out of these different traits. My goal was not to see which traits were more dominate in Jesus, or to try to create an exhaustive list of Jesus' activities and draw some kind of theological conclusion. My goal or charge was simply to watch and see how Jesus ministered to the people of His generation through His Father's personality.

It is important to note that Jesus didn't come to draw attention to Himself through His miracles, signs and wonders. He came to exemplify His Father, so He intentionally moved in the same way as His Father, as we read in the John 5:19 passage. He came to do what He saw His Father doing, and do it in like manner. You are to do the same. You are to discover the beautiful personality types that God has placed of Himself in you and use them in the same way, so as to exemplify your Father through the daily activities of your life.

Divine Dispositions

I made a list of a few of the Scriptures from the four gospels that reveal these five different personalities of God through Jesus' ministry. I have also included a few descriptions along with each passage that will help you identify the action verb associated with the personality type Jesus was demonstrating, or the reaction His activities produced. The words I put in *italics* serve as a reminder for you of the previous Greek definitions.

Jesus the Apostle

Matthew 4:18–22 Jesus *calls* the disciples.

Matthew 8:22—Jesus *calls* another disciple to follow Him.

Matthew 9:9 Jesus *calls* a tax collector to follow Him.

Matthew 10:5–20 Jesus *sends* out His disciples.

Matthew 28:18–20 Jesus *commissions* the disciples to "Go."

Mark 2:11 Jesus *commands* a paralytic, "Get up, pick up your pallet and go home."

Mark 3:3–5 Jesus *commands* a man, "Get up and come forward" and "Stretch out your hand."

Mark 3:13–19 Jesus summoned and *appointed* twelve disciples.

Mark 6:7–11 Jesus *sends out* His disciples in pairs.

Mark 14:13–15 Jesus *commands* two disciples, "Go into the city . . . prepare" for the Passover.

Luke 7:22 Jesus *commands* two of John's disciples, "Go and report to John what you have seen and heard."

Luke 8:54–56 Jesus *commands* Jairus's daughter to rise, and orders that something be given her to eat.

Luke 9:1–2 Jesus *commissions* the Twelve.

Luke 10:1 Jesus *commissions* the seventy to go out.

Luke 18:42–43 Jesus *commands* Bartimaeus, "Receive your sight."

John 5:8 Jesus *commands* a paralytic, "Get up, pick up your pallet and walk."

John 9:7 Jesus *commands* a blind man, "Go, wash in the pool of Siloam."

John 15:12 Jesus says, "This is My *commandment*, that you love one another."

John 15:16 Jesus says, "You did not choose Me but I chose you, and *appointed* you that you would go . . ."

John 15:26 Jesus says, "When the Helper comes, whom I will *send* to you from the Father . . ."

Jesus the Prophet

Matthew 9:4–5 Jesus *knew* the scribes' thoughts.

Matthew 12:25 Jesus, *knowing* the Pharisees' thoughts, responds.

Matthew 12:39–42 Jesus *prophesies* His death, resurrection and the coming judgment.

Matthew 22:18 Jesus *perceived* the malice of the Pharisees.

Matthew 24:4–31 Jesus *prophesies* the Tribulation and Second Coming.

Mark 5:30 Jesus *perceives* power leaving His body.

Mark 9:31–32 Jesus *foretells* His death.

Mark 11:14 Jesus *prophetically curses* the fig tree.

Mark 14:27–30 Jesus *prophesies* Peter's denial.

Mark 14:62 Jesus *foretells* His Second Coming.

Luke 5:22 But Jesus, *aware* of their reasonings, answers.

Luke 6:8 Jesus *knew* what they were thinking.

Luke 9:47 Jesus, *knowing* what they were thinking in their heart, responds.

Luke 11:17 Jesus *knew* their thoughts.

Luke 19:41–44 Jesus *prophesies* over Jerusalem.

John 1:47–51 Jesus *foreknew* Nathanael.

John 2:23–25 Jesus *knew* what was in man.

John 5:6 Jesus *knew* that the sick man "had already been a long time in that condition."

John 6:15 Jesus, "*perceiving* that they were intending to come and take Him by force to make Him king, withdrew."

John 6:60–65 Jesus was *conscious* of the disciples' grumbling and *knew* who did not believe.

Jesus the Evangelist

Matthew 4:23–25 Jesus went throughout all Galilee *proclaiming* the *gospel* of the kingdom.

Matthew 8:1 Large crowds *followed* Jesus.

Matthew 9:10–13 Tax collectors and sinners were *drawn* to Jesus, who says, "I did not come to call the righteous, but sinners."

Matthew 9:35 Jesus was "*proclaiming* the *gospel* of the kingdom."

Matthew 11:28–30—Jesus *draws* people, *proclaiming*, "Come to Me, all who are weary and heavy laden."

Mark 1:14–15 Jesus came into Galilee, "*preaching* the *gospel* of God."

Mark 1:38–39 Jesus *preached* in synagogues throughout Galilee.

Mark 1:45 People were *drawn* to Jesus even in the unpopulated areas.

Mark 6:56 Wherever Jesus entered villages, cities, the countryside or marketplaces, people were *drawn* to Him and He healed them.

Mark 10:1 He went to Judea and crowds *gathered* around Him.

Luke 4:43 Jesus said, "I must *preach* the kingdom of God . . . for I was sent for this purpose."

Luke 8:1 Jesus "began going around from one city and village to another, *proclaiming* and *preaching* the kingdom of God."

Luke 19:9–10 Jesus told Zaccheus, "Today salvation has come to this house," *proclaiming* salvation.

John 5:24 Jesus *proclaims* the Gospel, "Truly, truly, I say to you . . ."

John 6:27 Jesus *preaches* eternal life through the Son of Man.

John 7:37–38 Jesus *proclaims* the living water of God for all who will believe.

John 10:9—*Preaching* salvation, Jesus *proclaims*, "I am the door; if anyone enters through Me, he will be saved."

John 18:20 "I have *spoken openly to the world*," Jesus tells the high priest.

Jesus the Pastor

Matthew 9:36 Jesus *felt compassion* for the distressed and dispirited.

Matthew 14:27 Jesus *encourages* His disciples, "*Take courage . . . do not be afraid.*"

Matthew 15:32–38 Jesus *feels compassion* for the crowds and feeds them.

Matthew 19:14–15 Jesus *directs* the disciples to let the children come to Him.

Matthew 26:26–28 Jesus *serves* His disciples the Lord's Supper.

Mark 1:41–42 Moved by *compassion*, Jesus cleansed a leper.

Mark 5:36 Jesus *encouraged* the synagogue official, "*Do not be afraid* any longer, only believe."

Mark 6:34 Jesus had *compassion* on the crowd because they were like sheep without a shepherd.

Mark 8:6–8 Jesus *directed* the people to sit down, and He had His disciples *serve* them food.

Mark 8:23 Jesus *cared*: "*Taking the blind man by the hand*, He brought him out of the village."

Mark 10:51 Jesus had *compassion*, asking blind Bartimaeus, "What do you want Me to do for you?"

Luke 7:13 Jesus felt *compassion* for a mother whose only son had died and told her, "Do not weep." Then He raised him and gave him back to her.

Luke 13:12 When Jesus saw the woman in the synagogue who was bent double, He felt *compassion* and called her over and healed her.

Luke 18:15–16 Jesus *directed* His disciples, "Permit the children to come to Me."

John 3:16 Jesus told how God has *compassion*: "For God so loved the world . . ."

John 8:6–11 Jesus *forgives* the adulteress woman.

John 10:11–18 *Caring* for and *protecting* His sheep, Jesus says, "I am *the good shepherd*; the good shepherd lays down His life for the sheep."

John 11:33 Jesus felt *compassion* for the sisters of Lazarus, who had died, and "He was *deeply moved* in spirit."

Jesus the Teacher

Matthew 4:23—Going throughout all Galilee, Jesus *teaches* in the synagogues.

Matthew 5:1–48—Jesus *teaches* the multitude in His Sermon on the Mount.

Matthew 13:1–9 Jesus *teaches* a crowd from a boat.

Matthew 13:18–54 Jesus *teaches* in parables by the sea and in His hometown.

Matthew 20:1–16 Jesus *teaches* a parable about laborers.

Mark 1:21–22 Jesus entered the synagogue and began to *teach*.

Mark 2:13 Jesus *taught* by the seashore.

Mark 4:1–2 Jesus is *teaching* a large crowd from a boat.

Mark 6:1–2 Jesus *taught* at the synagogue in His hometown, Nazareth, and the people were astonished.

Mark 8:31 Jesus began to *teach* His disciples many things.

Luke 6:27–38 Jesus *teaches* rules of Kingdom life.

Luke 8:4–15 Jesus *teaches* the parable of the soils.

Luke 10:30–37 Jesus *teaches* the parable of the good Samaritan.

Luke 11:33–36 Jesus *teaches* the parable of the lighted lamp.

Luke 13:18–21 Jesus *teaches* about the Kingdom of God.

Luke 13:22 Jesus was *teaching* as He passed from one city and village to another on His way to Jerusalem.

John 3:5–15 Jesus *teaches* Nicodemus about being born again of the Spirit.

John 5:19–24 Jesus *teaches* about the Son's equality with God in power and authority.

John 7:14 Jesus went up into the Temple and began to *teach*.

John 8:1–2 Jesus *teaches* again in the Temple.

John 18:20 Jesus tells the high priest, "I always *taught* in synagogues and in the temple."

Along the Way

These are only a few examples of passages that describe Jesus exemplifying His Father's five personality types. Without much difficulty at all, I was able to attribute one of these five personality types to literally every action and reaction that Jesus exhibited in all four gospels. One of the most beautiful displays of Jesus' fluidity was found in John's account of Jesus' encounter with the woman at the well. I love this story because it represents an encounter that you or I could have on any given day. Maybe not at a well, but at a grocery store, a gas station, a salon, or waiting in line at a ball game. Jesus' encounters were often "along the way." They were not prearranged events or programs. They happened as everyday life happened.

Think about all the people your path crosses in a given day. Imagine if each of those encounters were an opportunity to share your Father's personality with someone who desperately needs to know Him. That's how Jesus lived here on earth. That's the way you and I need to be as we go about our day. Let's look at the story of the woman at the well, and I will point out in ten sections of passages what I perceive to be the different personalities of God as they emerge in Jesus' actions in John 4. All the scriptural verb or action phrases that appear in *italics* are my added emphases and give us the clues.

John 4:1–4

Therefore when the Lord *knew* [Prophet] that the Pharisees had heard that Jesus was making and baptizing more disciples than John (although Jesus Himself was not baptizing, but His disciples were), He left Judea and *went* [Apostle] away again into Galilee. And He *had to pass* through Samaria [Prophet].

I have categorized *knew* as the prophet personality, even though we don't know for certain if Jesus knew by getting word of the Pharisees' knowledge, or if He discerned it prophetically. Many scholars do agree, however, that Jesus knew or discerned that He *had to pass* through Samaria because of the awaiting divine encounter with the woman at the well. (Most Jews would not have passed through Samaria because they did not want to associate with Samaritans.)

John 4:5

So He *came* to a city of Samaria called Sychar, near the parcel of ground that Jacob gave to his son Joseph [Apostle].

When Jesus went anywhere, He was on assignment or under the commission of His Father. Whenever He went or came into a city or region, He was moving apostolically.

John 4:6

Jacob's well was there. So Jesus, being wearied from His journey, was *sitting* thus by the well [Teacher]. It was about the sixth hour.

Yes, Jesus was physically tired, but sitting was the rabbinic posture for teaching. We could conclude that He was not only resting, but also preparing to be used to teach whoever came to the well while He rested.

John 4:7–9

There came a woman of Samaria to draw water. *Jesus said to her*, "Give Me a drink" [Pastor]. For His disciples had gone away into the city to buy food. Therefore the Samaritan woman said to Him, "How is it that You, being a Jew, ask me for a drink since I am a Samaritan woman?"

Jesus valued this woman enough to associate with her and even to ask her for a drink. He demonstrates the humility and care of the pastoral personality of God. Pastors meet you right where you are in life and yet have the ability to give you loving direction!

John 4:10–12

Jesus answered and said to her, "If you knew the gift of God, and who it is who says to you, 'Give Me a drink,' *you would have asked* Him [Teacher], *and He would have given you* living water" [Pastor]. She said to Him, "Sir, You have nothing to draw with and the well is deep; where then do You get that living water? You are not greater than our father Jacob, are You, who gave us the well, and drank of it himself and his sons and his cattle?"

Jesus uses a teaching style here to draw out curiosity and to get the woman to think about what He has just said, so as to open the door to a deeper conversation. He adds to His statement a truth about His Father's Kingdom and makes it known that He would not hesitate in giving this precious gift to her. His ability to show her value and draw her out in conversation makes her engage with Him more deeply and ask more questions. She also then reveals and defends the basis of her Samaritan faith.

John 4:13–14

Jesus answered and said to her, *"Everyone who drinks of this water will thirst again; but whoever drinks of the water that I will give him shall never thirst; but the water that I will give him will become in him a well of water springing up to eternal life"* [Teacher/Prophet].

Jesus reveals a spiritual truth in a parabolic way using the water the woman draws every day, and He foretells of the living water's eternal ability and power.

John 4:15–16

The woman said to Him, "Sir, give me this water, so I will not be thirsty nor come all the way here to draw." He said to her, "Go, call your husband and come here" [Apostle].

The woman tries to avoid the deeper spiritual conversation by making an off-the-cuff remark. Jesus then makes a commanding, authoritative statement telling her to "Go" and get her husband. The apostolic personality of God motivates people to move, go, be sent or send.

John 4:17–20

The woman answered and said, "I have no husband." *Jesus said to her, "You have correctly said 'I have no husband', for you have had five husbands, and the one whom you now have is not your husband; this you have said truly"* [Prophet]. The woman said to Him, "Sir, I perceive that You are a prophet. Our fathers worshiped in this mountain, and you people say that in Jerusalem is the place where men ought to worship."

Jesus knows through divine understanding and discernment that this woman not only has no husband, but that she has had five.

John 4:21–24

Jesus said to her, "*Woman, believe Me, an hour is coming* when neither in this mountain nor in Jerusalem will you worship the Father [Prophet]. *You worship what you do not know; we worship what we know*, for salvation is from the Jews [Teacher]. *But an hour is coming, and now is*, when the true worshipers will worship the Father in spirit and truth [Prophet] . . . *for such people the Father seeks to be His worshipers.* [Evangelist] God is spirit, and *those who worship Him must worship in spirit and truth*" [Teacher].

This section of the conversation is the turning point. Jesus masterfully uses four traits in one powerful moment to get the woman to fully open her heart to truth.

John 4:25–26

The woman said to Him, "I know that Messiah is coming (He who is called Christ); when that One comes, *He will declare* all things to us." Jesus said to her, "I who speak to you am He" [Evangelist].

Jesus proclaims Himself to the woman at the well so that she can receive her Messiah.

Everyday Encounters

You can see from the ten sections of John 4 we just looked at how the five personalities of God are actively being displayed through Jesus' encounter with the Samaritan woman at the well. Now imagine what my Bible looks like, having worked through all four gospels! The pages are filled with the beautiful colors of God's personality through Jesus' intentional, Kingdom-focused actions and reactions.

You might be saying, "Well, that was Jesus and I'm not Jesus. I'm just a plumber [or a dentist, or an astronaut, or a politician or a songwriter]. I couldn't do *that*!" But, you can—if you allow the Spirit of God to work through you in your everyday encounters.

God's personality is not reserved for people who stand in pulpits! Jesus said that greater works than these you will do because He has gone to be with the Father (see John 14:12). He is looking to you and me to carry on the mission in *the same way* and in even greater ways. Jesus had these kinds of everyday encounters everywhere He went. And it should be the same for you and me, regardless of the river or rivers we are flowing in each day.

In the next chapter, you will discover your spiritual personality. I will let Laura walk you through it. You may think you already know what your spiritual personality is, but prepare to be amazed!

I believe that if a man wanted to walk on water, and was prepared to give up everything in life, he could do it.

Stirling Moss, British Formula One racing champion

Come On In,
the Water's Fine!

By now, you have read Chris's descriptions of the five personalities of God and have seen how Jesus flowed so fluently in them all, even in the course of one conversation with the woman at the well. And from me you have read about how each temperament thinks, feels and speaks, and you have seen them compared to moving bodies of water so you might better understand how you will flow into your river of influence (which you will discover in part two). In this chapter, it is now time for you to dive in and take your spiritual personality test.

I am glad we designated time in chapter 5 to examine various personality testing modules so that you will appreciate how they stack up to (or don't stack up to) the test you will take in this chapter. Those tests take a natural inventory of *your* personality, but our test will take a spiritual inventory of *God's personality in you*, which intimately and directly affects how others perceive you. It also affects how you can influence the world around you.

You probably already have a good idea by now about which of the five personalities of God you are dominant in. You may not be aware, however, of whether you are a hybrid of two or three. It is very important for you to be affirmed in these temperaments that you are already flowing in, plus learn the new ones you can awaken! You are about to be encouraged, relieved, inspired, released, and by the end of this book, commissioned.

Taking the Test

Chris and I have decided to ask you to go online to take your test for a couple of very important reasons:

1. It saves you time. The online test is an interactive quiz on a secure, personal website. The website will grade the test for you and immediately shoot the results to your email inbox.
2. It saves a few trees. It conserves paper in two ways since you don't have to supply your own paper for the test, and we don't have to include more pages in this book for you to write on.

Without further delay, go to the following link and answer the fifty multiple choice questions. Here is an example of what one looks like:

14. When someone does not do what I asked after I have already instructed them three times on exactly what to do, I:

a. become visibly and verbally upset

b. become upset but say nothing

c. do nothing; it does not bother me at all

d. don't care; I don't ever tell people what to do anyway

e. suggest we invite a new team member to help out

It should take you fifteen to twenty minutes to complete the test, and then we will send your spiritual personality results to you by email. Once you determine your river (or rivers), jump back into this chapter and we will talk about your personality flow a bit more. **Go to GoMakeYourSplash.com and click on Personality Test to begin.**

If you have finished your test and received your results, move on to the next section.

The Apostle Personality

Congratulations! You usually feel like the adult in the room. You have the innate ability to bring order to any situation, and the favor to convince the crowd to follow you. Chaos crumbles when you introduce your plan. Confusion flees when you explain the "why." And peace comes to everyone under your influence, which covers a lot of people since you have a knack for bringing others together. You are transparent and honest, but feel the weight of assuring everyone that things will be okay, even if you don't yet know how that will come about. You hear people's questions and fears in your head and can address those before they are asked. Even in a large crowd, you seem to be able to tap into corporate concerns and know the right thing to say and do. People trust you. Whatever your river of cultural impact is determined to be, you will quickly rise to the top there as a leader. Remember always to use your public sway for good. You can easily befriend all the other personality types, but are sometimes challenged by the take-charge prophet personality types (who need you). You are the apostle personality.

The Prophet Personality

Congratulations! You usually say what everyone else in the room wants to say, and then you get into trouble for saying it. As a result, you often feel both admired and rejected at the same time. You have eagle-eye discernment—more so than others around you—but you must remember that giving the right information at the wrong time will profit you nothing except for a pushy reputation with the people with whom you work and live. Even though you feel most valuable when you are having those "underground" revelatory experiences with God, resist the urge to be a loner. Instead, surround yourself with others to keep your moods steady. You must also surround yourself with affirming pastor personalities, which you are likely already doing instinctively. Don't be tempted to feel small in seasons of hiddenness. Just remember that God is bringing you more revelation during these times and will eventually provide you with the opportunity to release what you have seen and heard there. You are the prophet personality.

The Evangelist Personality

Congratulations! You are the spontaneous risk taker in the room, and often the most popular. You are the life of the party. You wear God's favor the way Joseph wore his coat of many colors that his father gave him. People love you—so much so that they find it hard to envy you when they otherwise would, due to your contagious smile and ability to win friends. And you love people back, but you have much more on your mind than winning friends. At your core, you are more interested in winning souls. In other words, you don't just love people in the present tense. You love them in the future tense and always have their eternity on your mind. Whether or not you are walking a full life with Jesus Christ, you are a natural salesman or spokeswoman and can influence crowds and rally audiences. You never stay in the shallow end of conversations. If you are a parent, make sure that you resist the urge just to be your child's friend. Make sure you embrace the authority and favor that is naturally yours. You are the evangelist personality.

The Pastor Personality

Congratulations! You are the kindest personality in the room. While many people have a pastor's heart, not everyone has the pastor personality. Sometimes, even an actual pastor in full-time ministry doesn't have the pastor personality. In short, you notice individual people and will pursue them one-on-one if you feel you can help them—much in the same way that a shepherd is willing to leave the 99 to go after the 1 lost sheep. And people hear you when you come, and what's more, they often come to you. While most people desire the Spirit's fruits of love and joy, you value the forgotten fruits of gentleness, faithfulness and kindness. Those come naturally to you. You are merciful and patient. You bear long with people and forgive easily. You also have the God-given ability to remove people's transgressions against you as far as the east is from the west. It drives some people around you crazy, especially the prophet personality types (whom you need). You are the pastor personality.

The Teacher Personality

Congratulations! You are the sharpest and perhaps smartest person in the room. Not because of a supernatural dispensation of wisdom, but because you have studied to show yourself approved. You are smart, but you don't store up knowledge to boast or pontificate. You store it up to share insights out of a motive to help others. You could teach to a crowd at a moment's notice (if you let yourself) and are always full of things to say. Not all teacher personalities are professional teachers, because remember, this is a personality trait, and it can find its way into any industry (river). The challenge for you is to avoid dominating all conversations, to remain teachable, and to make sure always that the knowledge in your head makes the twelve-inch journey down into your heart. Remember that the price for having the teacher personality and constantly being about the business of speaking into the lives of others is that you will be judged more strictly (see James 3:1). Bring those with the apostle personality into your inner circle so that you can observe the way they lead more by example and influence and less by pushy persuasion. You are the teacher personality.

Taking Inventory

Now that you know your dominant spiritual personality, you are almost ready to take inventory of your skills and talents and discover your river of influence. This will help you tremendously with occupational placement. Just one chapter left to go in this first part, in which Chris will tie up some loose ends that prepare you for part two. But since this is my last opportunity to help you prepare, I would like to end my final chapter in part one with a symbolic recap for you.

Just as we have given you the visual aid of how one drop of water starts in the skies, then goes to the mountaintops, then journeys down and becomes brooks, streams and rivers that eventually empty out into the oceans, I am realizing just now that that is the exact same journey Chris and I have been on while writing this book. Let me explain: We started out writing it in the mountains. We had gone to Denver, Colorado, where I would appear on the *Today with Marilyn and Sarah* show (Marilyn Hickey and Sarah Bowling). While there, we had decided to knock a few more states off our United States bucket list since we were getting so close to our final dozen states to visit. We extended our stay and decided to travel to Nebraska and Wyoming, come back through Colorado, and then travel all the way down to New Mexico. We had flown 1,150 miles from Nashville and were going to drive an additional 850 miles in our rental car.

We were stoked because we love traveling together and get to do it a bit more freely now as empty nesters. Plus, it was the perfect plan to isolate ourselves and begin this book, starting with the table of contents and mapping out each chapter. That is how we write, and how I suggest my online creative writing students write. Know the beginning, middle and end before you ever start.[1] So that was our plan. The table of contents was due to the publisher in a couple of days, and this was the perfect time for us to knock it out.

Maybe you don't have publishing deadlines, but you do have other type deadlines, so you can relate to how eager we were to execute our plan. We would even have lots of car time in which to get some good writing done. Right? Wrong. We had no idea what trouble awaited us the higher into the mountains we drove. I was fine in Denver at an altitude of 5,200 feet above sea level, and fine in southwest Nebraska at 5,400 feet. But the morning we woke up in Cheyenne, Wyoming, at 6,089 feet, I knew I was in trouble. What I thought was a mild case of food poisoning turned into one of the scariest few days of my life. But we had to stay on schedule, so we checked out of our hotel and headed south toward New Mexico, with me coming in and out of a daze.

The more we drove, the more it felt as if someone were sitting on my chest. Before long, I was losing coordination, was disoriented and couldn't even put on my own shoes. When a blizzard hit us near Colorado Springs, at still about 6,000 feet above sea level, we knew we were going to have to pull over. Not just for safety from the snowstorm, but because I was miserable and had now spiked a high fever. As it turns out, the closest thing right off the highway was a nice resort. Although it was gorgeous, spending the night would cost more than we typically spend on lodging. The higher we drove up the snowy mountain to the lodge, the stranger I felt. Once we were there, as Chris opened the drapes we realized that we were staring squarely at Pikes Peak outside our window, with an altitude of 14,000 feet above sea level.

I remember very little of the next two days, by the end of which we had deduced that I not only had a serious case of high-altitude sickness (HAS), but I also had high-altitude pulmonary edema (HAPE), and even high-altitude cerebral edema (HACE). High-altitude issues affect smaller people first, like children. I am only five feet two, so this sickness must have thought I was a kid! That explains why Chris developed symptoms later than I did, since he is larger than I am. One online article entitled "What Makes Different People More or Less Susceptible to Altitude Sickness?" reports that 25 to 85 percent of travelers to high altitudes experience altitude sickness. But don't worry, it's usually just mild symptoms that you can read more about in the article itself.[2] In addition to this, the National Library of Medicine website states that 81.6 million people live at higher altitudes and seem to experience genetic adaptations that help them adjust.[3] That would explain why residents of these beautiful states that we visited absolutely love living there and eventually experience none of these symptoms!

So there Chris and I were, unable to get down the snowy mountain for medical care. But being a naturopathic doctor, I was able to research the symptoms and we had every single one. We leaned on each other, and together we pushed a little loveseat up to the picture window, where we stared at the cumulonimbus clouds and snowcapped mountains where rivers are born. By God's grace, we mapped out for you what we now refer to as "the $600 table of contents." If we had to suffer, we at least suffered in style at the resort in the clouds, and hey, we met our deadline!

When we got to New Mexico, with regions of elevation at 8,000 feet, we turned in the table of contents and just lay in each other's arms and dreamed about sea level, especially about our home in Nashville, which is fewer than 600 feet above it. Immediately on disembarking from the plane in Nashville, I could walk with perfect coordination and take deep breaths, and Chris could breathe better, too. We still had a long recovery ahead due to the pleurisy and fever from the lung swelling, but we were happy to be home.

Now today, as I sit here writing this and am finishing up my portion of part one, I am staring at the ocean. We are in Newport, Rhode Island, which is a whopping thirty feet above sea level (thanks be to God)—a long way from that 14,000-foot elevated view of Pikes Peak that we were at when we started writing this book. So just as one drop of water comes from those types of mountainous skies and becomes a river and then an ocean . . . the writing of this book began on a snowcapped mountain and has ended at the sea as we close this chapter.

I started chapter 1 by explaining my regard for the seven mountain pioneer authors and teachers, and honestly, for the heaven-inspired concept itself. It remains timeless and true. In a sense, that mountain message made the way for this river teaching—much in the same way that mountains touch the heavens and receive the water that makes its way down to become the rivers that nourish all life.

Rivers know this: there is no hurry. We shall get there some day.
A. A. Milne, twentieth-century English author (of Winnie-the-Pooh)

10

Sink or Swim

Now Laura has helped you take the personality test, and you have learned something about yourself that maybe you did not know. And now, like my grandson Jad in the story from chapter 1, you are ready to say, "Yes, purpose!" You are convinced you have a purpose, and you are recognizing the spiritual personality God has gifted you with so uniquely.

Perhaps the idea of walking this out, however, seems as impossible to you as walking on water. Just remember, you are *flowing into* this river of influence, not being required to walk on it just yet.

While it should always be your goal to accomplish the miraculous in your future, for the time being focus on the two choices in front of you as you flow into your river(s) of influence: sinking or swimming. Let's take a look at how you do both.

Sinking 101

There have been many misrepresentations and misuses of God's personality types in the world and in the Church. There are leaders who use their apostolic gifts to control, manipulate and even harm the people they are called to lead. There are talented, creative people who use their voices and their creative expressions selfishly and pervert or twist the beautiful prophetic personality of God within them. There are communicators who use their evangelistic bents to establish platforms for personal influence and even political positioning. There are caregivers and public servants who pollute their compassionate acts and acts of service with greed and selfish gain. There are teachers who infect the minds of the innocent with toxic doctrines and politically laced ideologies. This is the sad reality of our fallen world.

But did you know that people who do not believe in God or desire to walk with Him relationally can exhibit portions of His personality? It's true. Like me, you may have encountered very successful people who are not the least bit interested in having a relationship with God, yet they carry leadership skills, wisdom and insight, have compassion, and even have great ability to teach. This is the reality of the world in which your river is going to flow. You will see evidence of God's personality even in people who have no interest in religion or a relationship with Him.

For instance, in my entertainment industry river years, my relationships were predominately with songwriters, singers and music artists. Every single creative person embodies the creative nature of God and will exhibit His *prophetic* personality, whether that person acknowledges God or not. Writers have the unique ability to hear silent words (if you are a writer, you know what I'm talking about), craft and convey thoughts, and speak in a voice that has the ability to capture people's attention.

The Greek word for *prophet* actually lists the poet, singer and musician as part of its definition of a prophet because of a creative person's ability to hear that which is not audible and to convey inspiration. Just imagine how that personality piece (or any other) could be used to benefit or impact the life of someone else when it is not being used selfishly, but intentionally in partnership with God. You and I can both make long lists of public figures and celebrities, however, who have risen to the top, and then have sunk straight to the bottom after a long, hard, public fall. They never discovered their true God-given purpose.

Sinking 102

I have worked with CEOs, VPs and owners of global companies. Some of them had a deep relationship with God, and others were not interested in a personal relationship with Him at all. Yet each of these leaders possessed the unique trait and skills of recognizing and directing talented people toward a specific mission, vision or cause. Now imagine the impact such leaders could have if they focused themselves on the purposes of God and focused their leadership gifts on the cause and mission of Jesus to bring hope and peace to the world. The world would look much different.

I have worked with super-talented sales and marketing people who could, without you knowing it, convince you to buy their brand like an evangelist calling in those in need of salvation. Imagine the impact these people could have if they embraced the purpose that God appointed for them and if they used their charisma to convince people to return to God. The world would be much different.

There have been teachers in my life who taught me about music, business and writing, and who mentored me in my journey as a pastor. Some of these teachers believed in God and some did not, but they all operated out of the teaching personality God gave them before they were born into this world. Imagine if every teacher understood the value of God's purpose in his or her life and could teach others how to discover their purpose, too.

I have encountered hundreds of people who, knowingly or unknowingly, cared for people out of the compassion that God placed in them before they were in their mother's womb. What if they all knew and operated in the full potential and genuine care of God? There would be a significant decline in destitution and hopelessness in the world.

You can find the personality of God in everyone because we are all His children. This is evidence to me of God's faithfulness and love toward all of His children. Unfortunately, most people are trained to rely on themselves, their talents, and their own wisdom and knowledge, and they have been deceived into abandoning the possibilities that exist through faith in God. So many well-intentioned people forsake God and eventually find themselves sinking in the turbulent waters of vanity, pride and unbelief. This reminds me of King Solomon's words in Proverbs 14:12: "There is a way which seems right to a man, but its end is the way of death."

Now, imagine if every single person whom God created knew that he or she possessed His personality and embraced His purpose. It would have an impact on literally every segment of society. This might seem like a pipe dream, but it is what God imagined from the beginning. He desires that all His children receive, enjoy and flow in His personality and purpose, because His personality and purpose produce the abundant life Jesus spoke of in John 10:10.

Swimming 101

What makes God's personality look different in someone who believes in Him and intentionally lives for Him than in someone who does not? The answer is twofold: the Holy Spirit and God's purpose. It has been my personal experience that when I choose to live intentionally under the leadership of the Holy Spirit and in pursuit of God's purpose for my life, I exhibit an uncanny joy and peace in the midst of the uncertainties of the world. I make choices and face decisions with faith, and I have an ability to live in hope for the future. The opposite was true of my life when I tried to live apart from God and in the confidence of my flesh. My countenance was dull. I gave in to fear and anxiety. I was much more self-focused and less others minded. The distinctions between my life apart from God and my life with God were as different as night and day.

We all have the choice as to whether or not, or at what level, we want God to be glorified through our lives. You can choose to glorify Him none, a little or all the way. You can sink or you can swim. The choice is yours, but the life that Jesus came to give you is a life destined to be lived to give God glory and to benefit the lives of others. It is a life of sacrifice.

In Matthew 5:16, Jesus said, "Let your light shine before men *in such a way* that they may see your good works, and glorify your Father who is in heaven" (emphasis added). True faith in God is a self-denying, not a self-promoting or self-glorifying lifestyle. It is a lifestyle that few are willing to choose because of the sacrifices involved, but it is a lifestyle that promises to add the most value to you. It is the "net worth" lifestyle I spoke of in chapter 4.

So, *how do* you live and work *in such a way* in a fallen world so as to glorify your Father in heaven?

There is only one way. I call it the *Holy Only Way*, or the *"HOW."* Living the *HOW* is mandatory if you are to exhibit a pure representation of God's personality to the world. If you try to express His personality traits in any way except a *Holy Only Way*, then you will likely mislead or hurt someone and cause damage to God's reputation in the process. You will sink in your river and make no impact at all. You have to get yourself out of the way and yield your body, your mind, will and emotions completely over to the Holy Spirit's leadership. You have to choose whether you are going to live *your way* or *Yahweh*! It is a lifestyle driven by the Holy Spirit (the *HOW*) with a God-centric purpose.

Swimming 102

Conveying God's personality to the world happens one action and reaction at a time. In every relationship and in every situation in your marriage, your family, your friendships and your professional and career relationships, you will either act or react out of your *flesh* or out of your *spirit*. Do not be deceived by your flesh! Your flesh will produce actions or reactions that may feel natural and even pleasurable in the moment, but they ultimately produce a variety of harmful outcomes for yourself and those around you. Galatians 5:19–21 (emphasis added) says,

> Now the deeds of the flesh are evident, which are: immorality, impurity, sensuality, idolatry, sorcery, enmities, strife, jealousy, outbursts of anger, disputes, dissensions, factions, envying, drunkenness, carousing, and things like these, of which I forewarn you, just as I have forewarned you, that *those who practice such things will not inherit the kingdom of God.*

When you are born again of the Spirit of God, however, you have the ability to produce actions and reactions that are synonymous with God's personality. Galatians 5:22–25 puts it this way:

> But the fruit of the Spirit is love, joy, peace, patience, kindness, goodness, faithfulness, gentleness, self-control; against such things there is no law. Now those who belong to Christ Jesus have crucified the flesh with its passions and desires.
> If we live by the Spirit, let us also walk by the Spirit.

It is my goal and desire, in my walk with Jesus, to glorify God in every situation. I know this is a tall order, and I am by no means perfect at it. Let me try to explain how I attempt to walk it out. When I am faced with an opportunity or a situation that requires me to act or react, I take in the information I am given, and then—in a split second, before acting or reacting—I try to process my feelings and make those feelings pass through my *HOW* Grid (remember, that means the *Holy Only Way*). I silently ask myself, *HOW do I feel right now? Do the feelings line up with my flesh or with the Holy Spirit?*

If my feelings side with the deeds or desires of my flesh, I try my best to hesitate, resist and stop. I take a silent deep breath, and then I make the effort to force those feelings through the *HOW* Grid to filter them before they become an action or a reaction. *Warning!* A sacrifice is required at this moment. My wife can tell you that I don't do this perfectly, but it is an exercise I try to set before myself in an attempt to live in such a way as to glorify God in every situation. As one who leads and directs people through God's apostolic personality, I must do it with gentleness and joy, so as to bring Him glory. When I care for people and serve them as a pastor, I must do it with love, peace and faithfulness, so as to bring God glory. When I am writing songs or even this manuscript, I must do it with faith, goodness and self-control, so as to bring God glory and not myself.

When I share my faith with people, I use the *HOW* Grid to make sure my approach is graced by the Holy Spirit and is kind, so they can feel loved and valued, and can sense the Father's presence. And when I teach others, I want to do it with patience and often long-suffering, so as to bring my Father glory. It is a split-second, conscientious act of surrendering the will of my flesh to the will of God's Spirit. This is the *HOW* to live in the personality of God and the *HOW* to flow in your river to the glory of God.

Flowing 101

Just as streams, underground waterways, tributaries, whitewater rapids and estuaries all flow into an ocean, *you* are going to take that God-given spiritual personality of yours and flow into your river of impact—and you are going to make quite a splash!

What is your river of influence? Are you ready to discover the twelve rivers of cultural impact and stick your toe in the one (or more) God has called you to? Pray this closing prayer with Laura and me, and then we will set sail.

Father God, I thank You that I have a purpose. I thank You that You have given me a unique piece of Your very personality, and I pray that I can mirror it brightly to this dark world. Thank You for helping me learn about both my purpose and my piece of Your personality in this first part, as well as identifying my natural gifts, acquired gifts and spiritual gifts. Thank You for revealing my "net worth"! I know now that I am useful to You on this earth. I will never again let anything convince me otherwise. Thank You that You have appointed a river of influence for me and have consecrated me to flow in it. I am ready to discover what it is! I am ready to flow into it. I am ready to swim, not sink. I am ready to turn the tide. Amen.

Either you decide to stay in the shallow end of the pool or you go out in the ocean.

Christopher Reeve, twentieth-century American actor (Superman)

Take the Plunge

Goals

1. For you to survey all twelve rivers and try to predict yours before part three's river placement test
2. For you to grasp God's perspective of each river's unique past and future
3. For you to discover Satan's history of polluting each river and help purify it
4. For you to gain God's protection in the river you are feeling pulled to enter (or are currently in)
5. For you to establish yourself as a person of eternal impact in that river

Part Two Subchapters

"Come to the River" Chris

"Hell or High Water" Laura

"Head above Water—Doctor's Orders" Laura

"The Coast Is Clear" Chris and Laura

"Walk on Water (from God's Word)"

What Is *Confluence?*

Confluence or *conflux* is the merging of two things. It is the place where two rivers converge, such as the Thompson and Fraser rivers in Lytton, British Columbia, or the Rhone and Arve rivers in Geneva, Switzerland, the Ohio and Mississippi rivers at Cairo, Illinois, the Rio Negro and the Rio Solimoes near Manaus, Brazil, the Drava and Danube rivers near Osijek, Croatia, and the Green and Colorado rivers in Canyonlands National Park, Utah.

Keep this picture of rivers merging in mind as you stick your toes in the waters of this part's twelve rivers of cultural impact. Study all twelve rivers, not just the one to which you assume you are called. You may feel a pull toward two different occupational rivers, and the reason could be that God is calling you to dive in and thrive in both. Here we go!

Home and Family River

You might be wondering why we are starting this part of a book on rivers of cultural impact with a chapter on home and family. In the following chapters, Laura and I will focus on marketplace rivers, and the first page of each chapter/river to come will be full of industry career paths for you. But we feel it is important to start here with the most important river of all—the family.

Let me explain. First, there is no influence that has been more impactful on you than your family, both positively and negatively. From the very beginning, God established marriage and family as the first institution through which humanity is to impact its culture. In Genesis 1:28, God blessed Adam and Eve with the charge to "be fruitful and multiply," and to "subdue" the earth and "rule over" His creation. There is no other institution in the earth through which God ordained this unique blessing. It was not given to an educational institution. It was not given to a financial institution. It was not given to a political or even a religious institution. God gave this responsibility to the family.

Second, it has been my personal experience as a pastor of nearly twenty years that the family is the single greatest area of spiritual attack by Satan and his armies. I have spent countless hours in premarital, marriage and family counseling over the years. I have spent more hours by far in this area of life counseling than any other. You see, we live in a culture predominately influenced by education, finance and career. We are trained at an early age to prepare for life through twelve years of secondary education, followed by two to eight years of post-secondary education in order to be successful. Sadly, most people never invest in a single hour of education about how to have a successful marriage and family.

We have allowed culture to steal God's purpose from the family, and we have willingly allowed other institutions to replace it. It is time to take back the family and reclaim its proper place in our lives and in society. Your home and family river will be God's most significant sector of impact for you. And even if you are single and live alone, hopefully you have friends and/or church family who are like parents and brothers and sisters to you. If you do not, make finding those people a priority in your life. Remember that God sets the lonely in families (see Psalm 68:6).

Come to the River

1. Where did this river start?

The family river started in a garden—the Garden of Eden. It was the origin of God's purpose and plan for the family. This Garden was a place of freedom and purity, a place designed for dependency on and faith in God. It was a sacred place. God created Adam and Eve and placed them in this Garden to be fruitful and multiply a godly legacy in the earth. In order to accomplish this, the institution of marriage required one man and one woman. God physically created them male and female so they could carry out this purpose. The unique and contrasting dynamics of the male and female relationship were intentional not only for physical multiplication, but so that the strengths of Adam could complete the weaknesses of Eve, and the strengths of Eve could complete the weaknesses of Adam. It was not good for Adam to be alone. He needed a helper, and God made a suitable helper for him in Eve. A counterpart. It was through the relationship of the first man and the first woman that the institution of family began. Like a river flowing out the Garden of Eden, the fruit of Adam and Eve began to populate the earth. Though sin and disobedience alter God's original plan and purpose for the home and family, His intentions have remained the same. The fruitful multiplication of a godly legacy in the earth happens when a man and a woman, as they value their unique differences, complete each other and become one flesh.

2. Where is this river going?

God created the family to have the ability to resist the sway of cultural influences through oneness with Him and oneness in the home. The oneness of a family devoted to God is to serve as a reflection of the unity that exists between the Father, Son and Holy Spirit in the earth. The family river that God ordained from the very beginning carries authority, yet runs with love, truth, forgiveness and hope. The family river is to flow into every segment of society with grace and light, its course unadulterated by the world and its influences. The home and family's course has been fashioned by God, and is to be directed exclusively by Him for His glory. Fathers will lead with confidence and humility. Mothers will be fruitful and nurturing. Children will honor, respect and bless their parents. This river is stirring, and there is healing in this river. Like a river flowing out of Eden, this river is designed to cause the remotest parts of the earth to bloom and bear everlasting fruit. But it will require a faithful devotion to God, through Jesus' redemption, and the grace and power of the Holy Spirit, to accomplish this. Are you ready to go where this river is going?

Hell or High Water

1. How has the enemy polluted this river?

There is much more than pollution in this river. There is blood, because family is blood. You won't hear me speaking so morosely about the pollution in the future river chapters, but the family river is much more than a world sector with industries and career paths. As Chris has already described, family is God's first institution established on earth. It flows everywhere and touches every other river. Even before the Church itself, God established the family in the Garden of Eden. Satan hates families because he doesn't have one, so he wants yours. But his goal is not to join it and feel the comfort he had before giving his heavenly family away when he rebelled against God and left them there. No, his goal is to join your family and absolutely destroy it. In fact, his job description is to steal, kill and then destroy, which we learn from John 10:10: "The thief comes only to steal and kill and destroy . . ." So we see that the enemy's thievery usually comes in this progression, and you may have even noticed it in your own family. He steals something from one relationship, maybe even something small. Without communication and forgiveness, he can then progress to the next step, which is to kill the relationship entirely. If no one in the family will intervene and mediate, his next plan is to utterly destroy—meaning the total destruction of your entire family tree. As any farmer will tell you, just one diseased twig can lead to a dead branch, and if not properly treated and pruned in such a way as to preserve life, it can kill the whole tree.

2. How can God purify this river?

Everyone is in this "industry," the home and family river. You were born in this river because you were born into a family. Even if you were given up at birth, or even if you leave your family by your own free will later in life, in God's eyes you are still in your family's river and can be used in it. Perhaps you have even added to its flow with a marriage and family of your own. You can help God purify this river by being aware of the enemy's job description and three-step progression plan we just discussed, and also by being aware of the statistics that prove he is busily working his plan. According to one article entitled "Are Divorce Rates in the U.S. on the Rise?" 50 percent of all marriages will end in divorce.[1] In the United States, second marriages will end in divorce 60 percent of the time, and third marriages have a 73 percent divorce rate. According to the U.S. Census Bureau, the top three reasons for divorce are incompatibility, at 43 percent, infidelity, at 28 percent, and money issues, at 22 percent. (While these statistics are specific to our country of America, many studies show that divorce rates have been increasing worldwide over the last fifty years.) People with strong religious convictions are 14 percent less likely to divorce, however, proving that they probably tackle these difficulties of incompatibility, infidelity and money issues with forgiveness and faith. So, help purify this river by doing everything within your personal power to remain a person of forgiveness and faith, so that such statistics will never darken your door.

Head above Water—Doctor's Orders

1. What are my health risks in this river?

Is being in a family hazardous to your health? The short answer should be no, but of course, there is always risk involved when you open your heart to someone. The easiest way never to be hurt is never to love at all, but how sad a life would that be? The reason that family wounds are the worst is because the people who can hurt you the most are the people who help and love you the most, or should. Think of it: The bag boy at the grocery store cannot wound your heart because he has no investments in it, nor do you have any expectations for him to be a guardian of it. Transversely, we *do* expect our family members to invest in our hearts, and at the very, very least, to guard our hearts for us. What do you do if you have family members who do not guard you or invest in you? Continue to invest in them the best you can. Pray big, and forgive even bigger. You may feel as though it is changing nothing, but I assure you that God is making note of it. He keeps good books and will eventually turn the tide in your favor if you have committed your course to Him. If a family member rejects you, it is his or her loss. If it is a sister, then God will send you a spiritual sister who will be more than you can ask or imagine. If it is a brother, God will bring you many spiritual brothers who will not reject you. If it is a child who has rejected you, just look around at the many spiritual children who *do* want you! But do these things without giving up on your blood family. Every family has problems, as evidenced back in the first family in the Garden of Eden, which resulted in one brother murdering another. Never forget that unless we want our family river to dry up entirely, we must daily try to bring cleansing to it in whatever way we can.

2. How can I protect myself in this river—body, mind and spirit?

Physically: Protect your family by vowing to God never to let domestic violence or sexual abuse enter your family through you.

Emotionally: If you see someone in your family who is drowning (in anger, unforgiveness or by entertaining false accusations), or someone who is drifting off alone into those dangerous waters, go after the person. Reason with and bring that person back in whatever way you can. And if you are the drifter, it is time to come home. With medical experts now agreeing that holding a grudge is one of the worst things you can do for your health because of how it prematurely ages you, my advice for all of us in this home and family river is to learn to forgive quickly and never get carried away into bitter waters. Consider the fact that God Himself put you into your family because *you* need them and they need *you.* Thus, the solution for the mucky familial waters you may sometimes find yourself swimming in is not to "flush" a family member out of your life. You are in a river, not a toilet. Follow the current through the ebb and flow that all relationships bring, and you will find that your family waters eventually run clear.

Spiritually: Commit your family to the Lord and make church attendance a weekly priority (or more often!) for you and your children. When they are older, encourage them to do the same with their children. It is true that the family that prays together, stays together.

The Coast Is Clear

How can my spiritual personality make an impact in this river?

The apostle personality: If you have the apostle personality, you walk into family gatherings with the estuary's ability to bring people together and find peace and unity. In fact, they may even be meeting in your home, but for sure, your entrance into a room brings a parental-type authority that can steady the waters and put everyone at ease. You carry yourself with loving wisdom, which can be useful to help carry your family in a positive direction. You may even be useful in your family as a mediator between members, should the need arise. Outside of family gatherings, you are the one who acknowledges and recognizes the giftings in your family members and encourages them to pursue the path where God can best to use them.

The prophet personality: If you have the prophet personality, you must walk into family gatherings "prayed up" so that you might be used by God prophetically while there, which is your desire. You seem to have an innate ability to know what others in the room are thinking, and you are definitely the feeler in your family. Becoming a loving, joyful encourager will open doors so that you might gain the necessary trust to speak into people's lives on a deeper level (like the underground river that you are). As God gives you dreams and visions for your family members, remember the story of Joseph and be very careful with your timing, lest it get you in trouble and get you thrown into a proverbial pit.

The evangelist personality: If you have the evangelist personality, when you walk into a family gathering the party finally begins. Your main motivation is to see people moving in the right direction with God, but it is not an agenda with you. You truly want to see them experience abundant life, both here and in eternity. You find yourself in a lot of deep, one-on-one conversations at family events, which is as it should be since you have the family reputation for speaking the truth in love. Should you be experiencing persecution because you are a minority in your family due to your gushing whitewater rapids revelations, just remember to let love lead the way so that others might see your heart, and more importantly, see the heart of God.

The pastor personality: If you have the pastor personality, when you walk into a family gathering you are asking what you can do to help. And even if you are busy with your children, you are training them to walk in and ask what *they* can do to help. Serving and making sure everyone's needs are met are your top priorities. It is an expression of love by you, even if you are not the host or hostess. In fact, you are likely one of the last to leave because you genuinely care that the hosts are not overburdened and left with a mess. Outside of family gatherings, yours might be the door that family members knock on for help during times of crisis, so stay ready for that and live your life in such a way that others trust your gentle stream of counsel.

The teacher personality: If you have the teacher personality, when you walk into a family gathering you might need to resist the urge to do all the talking since your tributaries are always full of insight. Instinctively and pure-heartedly, you want people to understand and have the necessary information on any given life topic, but just remember to do a lot of listening first so that your advice is relevant. People don't care what you know until they know that you care. Consider asking questions when in family conversations, so that people might see you are interested in what they have to say. Learning to affirm them will open their ears to your knowledge, which is plentiful and hard earned.

Walk on Water (from God's Word)

They drink their fill of the abundance of Your house; and You give them to drink of the river of Your delights.

Psalm 36:8

12

Information Technology River

Technology industries and careers include (but are not limited to) these:

Artificial intelligence technology
Computer-aided design software development
Conferencing service providers
Consumer drone manufacturing
Contact tracing systems
Contactless payment systems
Court reporting systems
Dark fiber network operations

Data backup software development
Data loss prevention software development
Data mining software development
Data recovery services
Digital advertising agencies
Digital forensic services
Document digitization services
Educational software development
Electronic access control system manufacturing
Electronic article surveillance manufacturing
Electronic automation software development
Endpoint security software development
Facial recognition software development
Fiber-optic cable manufacturing
Field service management software development
Fire and smoke alarm manufacturing
Fleet telematics systems
Fraud detection software development
Gas detection device manufacturing
Home automation services
HR and payroll software development
Hybrid and electric vehicle manufacturing
Identity management software development
Identity theft protection services
Internet hosting services
IT security consulting
Language learning software development
Learning software development
LED manufacturing
Live support chat
Metal detector manufacturing

Microprocessor chip manufacturing

Mobile payment service providers

Night vision equipment manufacturing

Online payment processing software development

Online survey software

Optical character recognition software development

Oscilloscope manufacturing

Podcast software development

Point of sale (POS) software development

Power circuit breaker manufacturing

Precision agriculture systems and services

Pressure sensor manufacturing

Real-time traffic information providers

Scrap metal recycling

Search engine development

Seismic monitoring equipment manufacturing

Smart meter manufacturing

Smart thermostat manufacturing

Smartphone app development

Social networking site development

Software testing services

Speech and voice recognition software development

Storage area network software development

Tax preparation software development

Traffic light manufacturing

Video conferencing software development

Video games software development

Virtual data rooms

Virtual reality software development

Wearable device manufacturing

Web analytics software development

Web design services

Web domain name sales

Website creation software development

Wireless Internet service providers

Come to the River

Long before the personal computer and the Internet were invented, God created you, my friend with the brilliant mind, to understand how to make information and technology work together to improve our lives. As you enter the river of information technology, the world is trusting you to use your ingenuity and problem-solving abilities to ensure that the information and processes you are inventing, managing and implementing are secure. The machines, the networks, the systems and their functionality will require the utmost in integrity as the world looks to you to make life easier, better and more enjoyable. Are you ready to make that kind of splash?

1. Where did this river start?

Since the beginning of time, humankind has been designing ways to make life easier. From the days when rocks were being used as hammers, knives and spears to our current era of information technology (IT) and artificial intelligence (AI), men and women have been in search of ways to advance productivity and share information. History timelines are often defined by the technologies that were invented during each cultural era. According to the *Encyclopaedia Britannica*, some of the technologies that have defined past eras of history include (in sequential order): fire, irrigation, sailing, iron, gunpowder, the windmill, the compass, the mechanical clock, printing, the steam engine, railways, the steamboat, photography, the reaper, the telegraph, the telephone, the internal-combustion engine, electric light, the automobile, the radio, the airplane, rocketry, the television, the computer, nuclear power, the transistor, spaceflight, the personal computer, the Internet, CRISPR (altering DNA), and artificial intelligence.[1] It's hard to

118

imagine life without these wonderful technological advancements. And many of the earliest technological advancements from history are still being used in some form today to make our lives easier!

2. Where is this river going?

With the ever-increasing growth of the IT sector, could we be living in the era described in the book of Daniel? "But as for you, Daniel, conceal these words and seal up the book until the end of time; many will go back and forth, and knowledge will increase" (Daniel 12:4). Laura and I believe that the "knowledge" is technology. "Tech-Knowledge-y!" So, the information technology river plays a huge role in the last days. With the speed at which information now travels, and with the ability of this information to perform tasks for us, we are living in a world that is becoming less and less physically demanding. The possibilities seem endless. But what will all this IT and AI do to our physical existence, besides making life easier? Will we all end up looking like those people floating around in carts in an interstellar city in the movie *WALL-E*? I pray not! If you are going to be floating in the information technology river, you get to help us decide. Enter *this* river with that thought in mind!

Hell or High Water

1. How has the enemy polluted this river?

As Chris just pointed out from the book of Daniel, God knew long ago that technology would increase in the last days. In that sense, God is not only the one who created the world, but also the one who created the World Wide Web! Many might see the evil that exists on the Internet and think that the enemy created it for his purposes, but the enemy creates nothing new. He is not the Creator, nor does he serve Him. Because of that, he can never be creative! His ideas are dull and lacking innovation. Instead, he has to stick to counterfeits. He has to piggyback on what God is doing and try to pervert it. In that sense, the only thing Satan can create . . . is trouble. For example, even as churches are using the Internet to broadcast God's Word through their livestreams, the enemy has tried to use that to lower church attendance and to separate and isolate the Body of Christ as its members forsake the assembling of themselves together (see Hebrews 10:25). But overall, it's easy to see why God would create a worldwide means for the fast dissemination of information: to spread the Good News of Jesus Christ! So then, seeing this genius invention, the enemy has merely decided to spread his bad news on the Internet, too: pornography, cyberbullying, online gambling, scamming, illegal downloading and content piracy, online predators, malware, identity theft, hacking, the loss of privacy, global cybercrimes, Internet addiction and the resulting health risks, which we will discuss in the "Doctor's Orders" section just ahead. But first, one final thought: Everyone wonders about the cryptic message in the book of Revelation that describes the mark of the beast being 666. We are given clues as to what that means, not just in God's Word, but *in the language itself* in which He wrote much of the Word, down to its very characters and letters. If the Jews are God's chosen people, then maybe Hebrew is God's chosen language. We see in it the unique distinction that each of its letters also has a numeric value. For example, if we look at 6, its alphabet counterpart is the Hebrew letter *waw*, or *w*. So that's right—the number 666 could easily translate to . . . *www*, the very letters that stand for the World Wide Web. Now read Revelation 13:17–18 (NIV) with that in mind:

> . . . so that they could not buy or sell unless they had the mark, which is the name of the beast or the number of its name.
> This calls for wisdom. Let the person who has insight calculate the number of the beast, for it is the number of a man. That number is 666.

We are definitely in the days where it is impossible to make certain purchases without the Internet. And with just the signing of a few bills and the flipping of a few switches, those people unwilling to use it will be totally unable to function in society.

2. How can God purify this river?

Despite all the enemy's pollutants, God has a plan for a Tech Revival. If you are feeling called to be in this information technology river, that plan includes you! Right in your cubicle, from your desk—or right in your home office, from your laptop—flows a river that has no boundaries and no pollution. With every boot, login and upload, you can help redirect the current of this IT river to flow in the direction God intends. That direction will bring life. Peace. Purity. Order. Protection. And so many more gifts God wants to pour out on His creation globally. This will happen with the content you create if you are a developer and designer, or with the hardware you create for it to all flow through, or with the manufacturing of other machinery if your skills are more tangibly technical. But never forget, God will also purify this river with your prayers as you learn to pray for it by the leadership of the Holy Spirit, and He will purify the other people in it as you make yourself available to them spiritually and impact their lives.

Head above Water—Doctor's Orders

1. What are my health risks in this river?

According to its website, Mobi Health News provides analysis, news and data to health innovators and pharma companies who are seeking to stay ahead of the sickness curve, to contextualize emerging health issues and to shape what's next in healthcare. In an article found there entitled "Lumo: 60 percent of workers have tech-related health problems," Mobi quoted Lumo Body Tech's cofounder and CEO as saying,

> Because our mission is to improve the health of humanity in this digital era, we think it's critically important for everyone who uses technology gadgets—at home and at work—to understand what this data says about technology and our health and to use this data as a call to action to adopt healthier tech usage habits.[2]

The Mobi article's writer went on to give these statistics:

For the Lumo study, Harris [International] polled 2,019 Americans 18 or older via an online survey. Findings suggested that eye-strain was the most common tech-related affliction, affecting 36 percent of Americans, followed by back pain (30 percent), neck pain (27 percent) and headaches (24 percent). Less common complaints included wrist pain (21 percent), carpel tunnel syndrome (11 percent) and insomnia (9 percent).[3]

I find it interesting that men were less likely to report their technology related health issues—only 56 percent of them, whereas 63 percent of women were reaching out for help. And the problem was better in the Northeast than on the West Coast—53 percent versus 66 percent respectively. As a company sparking innovation to help with these issues, Lumo also looked at how Americans treat their technology related health ailments. Believe it or not, 44 percent turned to medication for relief, whereas only 36 percent of people decided to just reduce their tech exposure. What's more, the article stated that "Those between 18 and 34 years old were more likely to take the time-reducing approach than their elders. They tried to cut down tech time 44 percent of the time compared to 29 percent of those aged 35 to 44 and 34 percent of those over 45."[4] These are just the physical risks, but we also know there are emotional hazards brought about by too much tech exposure, such as the negative effect on social relationships, the decrease in social skills, information overload, isolation depression, and even a decrease in cognitive development in young children who are constantly exposed to technological stimulation. Keep in mind that the above study was just for the general population . . . meaning that a career in technology comes with even greater health risks since it serves a reason that you would have even more tech exposure in this industry day in and day out.

2. How can I protect myself in this river—body, mind and spirit?

Physically: If you work on a laptop, buy a heat and radiation resistance panel to lessen continual radiation exposure (like the

HARApad I use, for example). Set screen time and work boundaries that limit your tech engagement. If you work at a desk, try to get outside once a day for an "air bath." Take just a brief walk that will clear your mind, fight weight gain and nourish your lungs, bringing oxygen and energy to your whole body. Watch your posture as you sit, and protect your core organs by resisting the urge to slouch constantly. Prevent dry eye and other optical issues by using blue blocker lenses.

Emotionally: Never let an app replace a human being.

Spiritually: Prayerfully "ordain" your devices and equipment to God and watch them function better and last longer. (This has worked for me for decades).

The Coast Is Clear

How can my spiritual personality make an impact in this river?

The apostle personality: If you have the apostle personality, then you have the God-given ability to lead, direct and bring order. Depending on which season and position you find yourself in at your place of employment in the technology industry, you should expect that your future will include organizing, directing and commissioning people into roles and responsibilities. Like the Roman centurion in Matthew 8:5–13, be a person of authority and a person *under* authority. Then promotion and favor will find you. Wherever you are, be that estuary and tap into your God-given ability to bring people together, promote unity and solve problems using the hi-tech mind God has given you.

The prophet personality: If you have the prophet personality, you may be the one who often sees trouble coming at work, whether it be in various tech projects or in interpersonal staff relationships. But that means you may also be the visionary team member who is called on to inspire others and bring new innovations to the table. Positive or negative, test the things that you hear with prayer and submit them when possible. And remember, package your white-water rapids passion in such a way that you can be heard by all.

You will never be short on ideas, so you want to make sure that you are able to follow through with everything you start. Also be open to the idea that you may be the one whom God alerts to create (or work with someone who can create) new technological safety protocols that will protect people, their homes, businesses, assets and even their civil liberties, depending on your tech field.

The evangelist personality: If you have the evangelist personality, then you are not afraid to be in front of people. This may land you in positions of sales, marketing, publicity and other more frontline rallying roles in the tech world. Don't limit God. Let Him take you to the people He wants to reach through you, regardless of whether you are the president, the project manager or the programmer. Outside the office—especially if you have to work with the public—remember that your next customer might also be your next assignment from the Lord. In that case, you will have to lead with your heart and not just your brain, which you don't always give yourself permission to do.

The pastor personality: If you have the pastor personality, whether you are the director, the developer or just the digital jack-of-all-trades, yours is the office or cubicle that others will enter to discuss their problems. Either that, or you are the phone call they will make when they know they are in over their heads. This can involve a technical project, a staff issue or a personal crisis. You are the heart in an industry full of brains. You take time for these people because you understand that it creates a better business overall when they are cared for. Because of this, and because you work well with others, you will gain a good reputation fast and be trusted with greater responsibility.

The teacher personality: If you have the teacher personality, no matter which sector of tech infrastructure you are in, you possess the ability to communicate complicated and sophisticated ideas and make the complex understandable. From a very early age, you have had a mind that solves problems and even technical challenges. Yet don't become so internally focused that you forget that there are others who need your knowledge, and sometimes just a helping hand. You will be the one called on to make the technical practical, and you will always face the challenge of working with people who know less than you do, which will require a great deal of patience on your part. To be used by God to the fullest in this industry, you will often have to allow your heart to override your brain.

Walk on Water (from God's Word)

For thus says the LORD:
"Behold, I extend peace to her like a river,
And the glory of the nations like an overflowing stream."

Isaiah 66:12 ESV

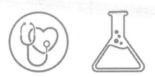

Healthcare and Therapeutic Sciences River

Healthcare and therapeutic sciences industries and careers include (but are not limited to) these:

Acupuncturists

Adoption and child welfare services

Adult day care

Air ambulance services

All pharmaceutical medicine manufacturing

Allergists

Alternative healthcare providers

Ambulance services

Ambulatory surgery centers
Anesthesiologists
Animal health biotechnology
Animal pharmaceuticals
Artificial joint and limb manufacturing
Assisted living facilities
Audiologists
Behavioral therapists
Biotechnology
Blood and organ banks
Blood banking and tissue typing facilities
Blood testing services
Cardiologists
Cell therapy
Children's specialty hospitals
Chiropractors
Clinical trial data management services
Clinical trial support services
Coffin and casket manufacturing
Compounding pharmacies
Contact lens manufacturing
Contract pharmaceutical research services
Corporate wellness services
Cosmetic dentists
Cremation services
Crisis intervention services
Cryogenic biobanking services
Defibrillator manufacturing
Dental clinical instrument manufacturing
Dental equipment dealers
Dental laboratories

Dentists

Dermatologists

Diagnostic and medical laboratories

Diagnostic imaging centers

Dialysis centers

Dialysis equipment manufacturing

DNA and DNA forensic laboratories

Drug and alcohol rehabilitation clinics

Drug and alcohol test kit manufacturing

Ear, nose and throat hospitals

Eating disorder clinics

Elderly and disabled services

Electronic medical records systems

Emergency and other outpatient care centers

Emergency veterinary services

EMT/paramedics

Endocrinologists

Endodontists

Endoscope manufacturing

Essential oil research and manufacturing

Eye health products

Eye surgery clinics

Fertility clinics

Foot care product manufacturing

Forensic technology services

Geneticists

Gerontologists

Glucose meter manufacturing

Gynecologists and obstetricians

Hair loss treatment manufacturing

Health and wellness spas

Health coaches
Healthcare and social assistance
Hearing aid clinics
Hearing aid manufacturing
Hearing protection equipment manufacturing
HMO providers
Home care providers
Homeopathic treatment production
Homeopaths
Hospices and palliative care centers
Hospital bed manufacturing
Hospitals
Human biologics manufacturing
Immunodermatologists
Infectious disease specialists
Institutional pharmacies
Intravenous (IV) hydration centers
Laboratory casework manufacturing
Laboratory glassware manufacturing
Laboratory information management systems
Mammography machine manufacturing
Mammography services
Medical adhesives and sealants manufacturing
Medical case management services
Medical device cleaning and recycling
Medical equipment repair and maintenance
Medical transcription services
Medical waste disposal services
Memory care providers
Mental health and substance abuse centers
Midwives and doulas

Mobility equipment stores
Natural disaster and emergency relief services
Naturopaths
Nebulizer manufacturing
Neonatal physicians
Nephrologists
Neurologists
Neuropathologists
Nurse practitioners
Nursing care facilities
Nutritionists and dietitians
Occupational health and workplace safety
Occupational therapists
Oncologists
Ophthalmic equipment dealers
Ophthalmic instrument manufacturing
Ophthalmologists
Optometrists
Organ and tissue donor services
Orthodontists
Orthopedic products manufacturing
Orthopedists
Orthotic manufacturing
Osteopaths
Otologists
Pacemaker manufacturing
Pain management physicians
Pathologists
Pediatric dentists
Pediatricians
Periodontists

Personal trainers

Pet funeral and cremation services

PET scanner manufacturing

Pharmaceutical manufacturing

Pharmaceutical research

Pharmaceutical wholesaling

Pharmacy benefit management

Physical therapists

Physical therapy rehabilitation centers

Physician referral services

Plastic surgeons

Podiatrists

Primary care doctors

Proctologists

Prosthetics manufacturing

Protective eyewear manufacturing

Psychiatric hospitals

Psychiatrists

Psychologists

Pulmonologists

Radiologists

Residential intellectual disability facilities

Respiratory ventilator manufacturing

Retina specialists

Retirement communities

Rheumatologists

Robotic surgery equipment manufacturing

Sleep disorder clinics

Specialist doctors

Specialty hospitals

Speech-language pathologists

Sports medicine practitioners
Stent manufacturing
Surgical apparel manufacturing
Surgical instrument manufacturing
Syringes and injection needle manufacturing
Teaching hospitals
Telehealth services
Toxicology laboratories
Urgent Care centers
Urologists
Veterinary medicine
Weight loss surgery centers
Wheelchair manufacturing
Wildlife rescue and rehabilitation
X-ray machine manufacturing

Come to the River

You who have a deep empathy for the care and well-being of others, understand that this river carries with it one of the greatest opportunities for representing the heart of God in the earth. With your ability to research, invent medical devices, communicate, administrate and provide treatment out of compassion for others, you will be connecting with people in their greatest hours of need. In Exodus 15:26, God reveals Himself this way: "I, the LORD, am your healer," which is *Jehovah Rapha* in Hebrew. This passage describes who God *is*, not simply what He *can do*. So, as you migrate into the river of healthcare and therapeutic sciences, go with the understanding that you carry the very essence of who God *is*—the Healer! In this river, people will be entrusting their very lives to your care, counsel, inventions and treatments. And if you are a veterinarian, you have the same exact calling, except to God's creatures! Your skills in communication, teamwork and ethics are essential components to your education and training in this river.

1. Where did this river start?

Along with over 24.3 million people in the United States[1] and 59 million people worldwide,[2] your empathy for others will build on the work of some of the most curious and compassionate names in medical and healthcare history. Names like Hippocrates (450 BC), Claudius Galenus (AD 130), Leonardo da Vinci (the 1400s), Anton van Leeuwenhoek (the 1600s), Louis Pasteur (the 1800s), and even Earle Dickson, who invented the Band-Aid in the 1920s for the Johnson & Johnson company. You will be jumping into this river with other talented, devoted, compassionate caregivers, doctors, inventors, technicians, chemists, therapists and naturopaths to demonstrate God's care and compassion to people with a variety of healthcare needs. As far back as 1445 BC, God instructed Moses to fashion a staff made of bronze with the image of a serpent wrapped around the pole, and anyone who had been bitten by a snake in the desert was to look at the staff and be healed (see Numbers 21:6–9). This image is still used on ambulances and hospitals today as a symbol of healing. Remember that this symbol originated with the Great Physician.

2. Where is this river going?

As advanced as your healthcare river is and will become, there will never be a replacement for empathy. It will be important for you to keep your heart at the center of your research, your care, your communication and your teamwork. As more and more emphasis is put on the treatment of *symptoms* by doctors and pharmaceutical companies, there is a growing need for *cures*. Believe God for witty inventions (see Proverbs 8:12 KJV), and for healing therapies and even miraculous interventions. God needs caring souls to bring His healing care to a world that so desperately needs it. As long as there are people and pets, there will be a need for your empathy, ingenuity and integrity. As people entrust their lives and loved ones to you, know that they are not just looking for a remedy; they are looking to you for hope. To be successful in this river, you will have to flow with the heart of God.

Hell or High Water

1. How has the enemy polluted this river?

Plain and simple, through corruption. The National Academy of Sciences released one study entitled "The Critical Health Impacts of Corruption." Their "Key Findings" on the pollution of what should be a life-giving river are staggering. I want to list them for you here in their own authoritative words:

- Approximately $455 billion of the $7.35 trillion spent on health care annually worldwide is lost each year to fraud and corruption. Furthermore, the Organisation for Economic Co-operation and Development estimates that 45 percent of global citizens believe the health sector is corrupt or very corrupt.

- Globally, 1.6 percent of annual deaths in children under 5—more than 140,000 deaths—can be explained in part by corruption.

- Chronic government underfunding, insufficient regulatory oversight, and lack of transparency in governance can breed corruption and reduce the quality of health care.

- Public spending for health care is inefficient in countries with poor governance. Good governance, on the other hand, is vital for national health care systems to work optimally. In fact, the quality of governance is a key mediator for whether public spending on health care influences health outcomes positively.

- Many strategies exist for reducing corruption and making environments less conducive to malpractice, including remunerating health care workers adequately, adequately financing the public health care system, ensuring social accountability, and strengthening institutions outside the health care sector.[3]

134

2. How can God purify this river?

Simply put, our world needs revelation of the fact that God is the Great Physician. As man has tried to leverage himself as the Healer (which even I as a naturopathic doctor agree that no doctor can be), pride and corruption have polluted this river and have prevented true healing from flowing in it. As a result, our "healthcare" industry has become more like "disease maintenance," and not healthcare at all. Aside from a healing revival, there are some very practical ways that we can curb mankind's power over a sector that really should be more about relationship with God and less about industry. Here are a few of them from the previously quoted study:

- Transparency in pricing of medical supplies at hospitals in Argentina resulted in a 50 percent decline in price variation across hospitals [a strategy applicable elsewhere].
- Social accountability mechanisms, such as user-centered information systems, citizen monitoring, public grievance and redress, and even participatory budgeting, have been found to improve health outcomes in various settings.
- Hiring of outside individuals with no ties to a corrupt institution can roll back vested interests and create an impetus for positive change.[4]

The article concludes that societies and their governments need more transparency and safeguards—both inside and outside the healthcare industry—so that we might see an increase in health and a decrease in corruption overall.

Head above Water—Doctor's Orders

1. What are my health risks in this river?

Aside from the obvious risks of the constant exposure to disease for anyone in the healthcare industry, my number one concern is for hospital and medical staff, because of your consistent sleep deprivation. I first became aware of this problem while writing my book *Seeing the Voice of God: What God Is Telling You Through Dreams and Visions* (Chosen, 2014). I interviewed Dr. Jonathan G. W. Evans, M.D., a board-certified pulmonologist at the Middle Tennessee Pulmonary Associates at Skyline Medical Center in Nashville, Tennessee. (Pulmonologists study to resolve, among other maladies, sleep disorders such as sleep apnea.) Evidently, after medical school the newest doctor graduates completing internships often must work back-to-back shifts of 24 to 36 hours with little or even *no* sleep. In fact, Dr. Evans began our interview with a voluntary testimony about his own sleep debt during medical school and about how it didn't improve during his residency. He told the story of how for three solid years he worked grueling 36-hour shifts, which were, in his own words, "interrupted by 0–3 hours of fragmented sleep." At the end of those 36 hours, he would sleep hard for 11–12 hours and then repeat the cycle. This meant that most weeks he worked 120 hours! What I was most astounded by was that after all of that, he went on to specialize in sleep medicine during his fellowship at George Washington University. Perhaps it was because he had a newfound appreciation for sleep! I also learned something interesting from a study led by Dr. Charles Czeisler from Harvard Medical School's Division of Sleep Medicine. Entitled "Sleep, Performance, and Public Safety," the study found that hospitals could reduce their medical mistakes and oversights by an outstanding 36 percent by limiting doctors' shifts to no more than 16 hours at a time, with a weekly workload not to exceed 80 hours.[5] Dr. Evans echoed this during our conversation, stating that just a few years after he graduated, studies were done that prompted government intervention to regulate hospital shifts, promptly ending such marathon rotations.

2. How can I protect myself in this river—body, mind and spirit?

Physically: Whether you are a doctor or a hospice worker or an in-home caregiver, make sure that rest is at the top of your list in caring for yourself physically. Accept no job that harms your health when you yourself are trying to bring health to others.

It's counterproductive! If you are one who works with healthcare equipment in departments like radiology, make sure you wear proper protection. And if you are constantly exposed to diseases, bolster your immune system with extra nourishment in the form of eating greens every single day. Do this as if your life and health depend on it, because they do! God has put within the leaves of our plants and herbs both the preventions and cures for everything that ails humankind: "Then God said, "Behold, I have given you every plant yielding seed that is on the surface of all the earth, and every tree which has fruit yielding seed; it shall be food for you" (Genesis 1:29).

Emotionally: Remember to practice tiny acts of self-care when the stress of caring for others gets to be too much. One of my very first jobs as a newlywed was as a medical transcriptionist, and there were times when I thought I would go stir-crazy just having a desk job in the healthcare industry! (At the time, I looked at it as a secretarial/assistant type job, but now I see that learning all those medical terms was part of God's plan for me in the future as a naturopathic doctor.)

Spiritually: Be a person of integrity in this industry that is so overrun by corruption. From desk clerks to doctors (including veterinarians), from pharmaceuticals to forensics, try to live by the Hippocratic oath, which can be summed up with the words "do no harm." Remember that you are really serving the Great Physician, and that no matter what your job in this industry, you do everything unto Him.

The Coast Is Clear

How can my spiritual personality make an impact in this river?

The apostle personality: If you have the apostle personality, leadership will find you no matter where you start out in this industry. If you are at a desk job, you already have your eye on a bigger desk. If you are part of a hospital staff, you already know exactly which floor you want to be on—or be in charge of. If you are a caregiver or a health spa professional, this spiritual personality type is a born entrepreneur. A self-motivated problem solver and uniter, you are the estuary that brings teams and their ideas together. Just remember that in an industry known for teamwork, you will have to work your way through the ranks and become well acquainted with every post along the way. But this also will give you great authority wherever you are going, or knowing you, where you already currently are.

The prophet personality: If you have the prophet personality, you see everything that is wrong with this industry, starting with your own department, wherever you are. Your first calling as the underground river is to pray deeply for those in leadership over you, for those you are leading, or both. Secondly, when you think you have a solution—which you often will—make sure to remember that you are a team player and that someone in authority over you may have the final call. Since you are gifted with intuition and innovations, you can expect God to give you new ideas, big and small, that will not only be a blessing to those you work with, but also to the many patients you corporately serve. They are waiting for you to revolutionize your industry.

The evangelist personality: If you have the evangelist personality, you see the patients and clients you serve through an eternal lens. Whether you are a cosmetic dentist or a coffin maker, your hands are in your work, but your head is in the skies. You are always looking for opportunities to share your faith, so remember never to accept a position that stifles this God-given whitewater rapids personality in you. At your core, you want to save lives, but that is merely a picture of how you desperately want to save people from eternal separation from God. With the favor and charisma that seem to come to you so effortlessly, you will never be satisfied with a behind-the-scenes job.

The pastor personality: If you have the pastor personality, then every day you get up and put on empathy in the same way that a doctor puts on his white coat, a radiology technician puts on her vest, or an eye health professional helps people put on their new pair of glasses. You feel the pain of others, and your main priority is their comfort, care and healing. And you see their faces, even if you don't work directly with people in your area of expertise. On your team, it is these very characteristics that will attract others to you with their needs, secrets and prayer requests. Your heart is always on call. Your words are like the nourishment of a gentle stream to a parched land.

The teacher personality: If you have the teacher personality, you will constantly be pouring into others with your skill. Because of that, you will always have to be aware of sharpening your interpersonal skills and communication strengths and weaknesses. You find pleasure in teaching others what you know, no matter where you are in the chain of command in your industry. Remember, the word *doctor* comes from the Latin *docēns*, which literally means "to teach."[6] Whether you are an audiologist or an activities director in a nursing home, your heart will always be as full as a multitasking tributary to teach those in your care in such a manner that when they leave your presence, they feel as though they have been cared for by the Healer Himself.

Walk on Water (from God's Word)

By the river on its bank, on one side and on the other, will grow all kinds of trees for food. Their leaves will not wither and their fruit will not fail. They will bear every month because their water flows from the sanctuary, and their fruit will be for food and their leaves for healing.

Ezekiel 47:12

14

Politics and Law River

National and international political and law industries and careers include (but are not limited to) these:

Global Government Branches:
Bi-/multi-/tetra-/tri-/uni-cameralism
Chancellors
Chief executives
Chief ministers
Constitutional court
Executive (presidents)
First ministers
Heads of State

Judiciary

Legislature (Congress; Parliament)

Lower House/Upper House

Monarchs (kings or queens)

Nonpartisan Democracy

Party systems

Premiers

Prime ministers

Supreme Court

Supreme leaders

Connected Industries:

Constitutional law

Democratization

Economics

Ethics

Foreign intelligence

Foreign policy analysis

Geopolitics and political geography

Globalization studies

History

Institutional theory

International legal theory

International relations

Jurisprudence

Multilevel governance

Nationalism studies

New institutionalism

Polarization

Policy analysis and policy studies

Political activism

Political anthropology
Political history
Political jurisprudence
Political philosophy
Political psychology
Politicization
Post-nationalism theory
Psephology—study of elections
Security studies
Social science
Sociology
Voting theory

Connected Careers:
Attorneys (see the next list for types)
CIA agents
Campaign managers
Campaign staffers
Diplomatic service officers
Government social research officers
Legislative or congressional aides
Lobbyists
Personnel security specialists
Policy analysts
Political activists
Political assistants
Political pundits
Political staffers
Pollsters
Press secretaries
Public opinion analysts

Secret Service agents

Special interest advocates

Speechwriters

National and International Law:

Associate attorneys

Attorney generals

Background check services

Bankruptcy lawyers and attorneys

Benefit administration services

Business lawyers and attorneys

Child adoption agencies

Claims adjusters

Consumer lawyers and attorneys

Corporate law firms

Court reporting (stenography)

Criminal lawyers and attorneys

Customs brokers

Debt relief services

Defense attorneys

District attorneys

Divorce lawyers and attorneys

Employment law firms

Entertainment lawyers and attorneys

Estate lawyers and attorneys

Family law

Foreclosure lawyers and attorneys

Healthcare lawyers and attorneys

Immigration lawyers and attorneys

Injury lawyers

Insurance lawyers and attorneys

International law firms
Judges (elected and appointed)
Judicial clerks
Labor relations lawyers and attorneys
Legal assistants
Legal file clerks
Legal interns
Legal receptionists
Legal secretaries
Litigation attorneys
Mediation services
Medical malpractice agencies
Online mortgage brokers
Online stock brokerages
Paralegals
Patent attorneys
Personal injury lawyers and attorneys
Prosecutors
Public defenders
Real estate law firms
Repossession services
Settlement funding companies
Stenographic services
Tax lawyers and attorneys
Trademark and patent lawyers and attorneys
Transcription services
Trial lawyers

Geopolitical Streams:
Please note that since this is a global book, we want to give a balanced representation of all global governments and their geopolitical offshoots. We also list them here because God desperately

wants to shine a bright light inside each one of these streams of thought. So if you are called to this politics and law river, you may find yourself influencing those within these geopolitical offshoots with your Christian beliefs.

Anarchism

Anti-Revisionism

Athenian Democracy

Autonomism

Blue Water Thesis

Consent of the governed

Critical International Relations Theory

Decoloniality

Deliberative Democracy

Democratic Peace Theory

Democratic Theory

Direct Democracy

Functionalism in international relations

Hegemonic Stability Theory

Idealism in international relations

Individualist anarchism

International Relations Theory

Islamic State

Left Communism

Liberalism (international relations)

Majoritarianism

Maoism

Marxism-Leninism

Marxist International Relations Theory

Metapolitics

Nationalism

Neomarxism

Neoliberalism

Neorealism

Participatory Democracy

Patriotism

Peace and conflict studies

Political geography

Political symbolism

Post-colonialism

Power Transition Theory

Power in international relations

Radical Democracy

Realism in international relations

Referendum

Representative Democracy

Republicanism

Secession

Social anarchism

Social contract

Sovereignty

Structural Marxism

The Frankfurt School

Theories of State

Third-worldism

Three-world model

Trotskyism

Come to the River

You who have a heart for justice and a mind equipped with an ability to conceive and establish laws that benefit, protect and govern people with equity, God has appointed and consecrated you to bring integrity and morality into the political and legal systems of the world today. As the world desperately tries to redefine morality and ethical behavior, your backbone will have to be unwavering as you dive into the brutal waters of politics and law.

1. Where did this river start?

Hammurabi was king of the First Babylonian Dynasty in the Middle East from 1792–1750 BC. He is credited for writing one of the earliest known laws in history. As the History Channel tells us, "Hammurabi's Code is one of the most famous examples of the ancient precept of 'lex talionis,' or law of retribution, a form of retaliatory justice commonly associated with the saying 'an eye for an eye.'"[1] The Bible cites Moses as the first judge in Israel's history as the Israelites wandered forty years in the desert (see Exodus 18:13–22). He was followed by a delegation of "able men who fear God, men of truth, those who hate dishonest gain," to assist him in settling disputes (verse 21). Deborah, a prophetess, was among the first judges established in Israel after Joshua's conquest of the Promised Land, prior to Israel's establishment of a monarchy under King Saul. The first and only female judge mentioned in the Bible, Deborah rendered her judgments from under a palm tree in the mountains of Ephraim (see Judges 4:4–5). Along with Deborah, the book of Judges records eleven other judges assigned for the task of settling matters of the law: Othniel, Ehud, Shamgar, Gideon, Tola, Jair, Jephthah, Ibzan, Elon, Abdon and Samson. The need for laws in civilization has been universal. History has taught us that lawlessness cripples a nation. Since personal ethics are not enough to maintain order in society, the river of politics and law must continue to flow from history into our lives today. And wherever laws and policies are being considered, you can be assured that there will be a need for lawyers, politicians and judges.

2. Where is this river going?

As lawyers, public servants, and businessmen and businesswomen from a wide variety of backgrounds wade into the waters of politics and law, this river has become a melting pot of social and political ideologies that has drowned even the most well-intended of lawmakers. Swimming upstream in this river will not be respected, but it will be necessary. Be forewarned, this river's current flows under the influence of the most powerful and influential people in the world. And the currencies that control these currents no longer bear the motto "In God We Trust." Turning over the tables of injustice in politics and law will require an unwavering faith and a connection to many unwavering, faithful colleagues. God is looking for men and women who will meet the qualifications outlined by Moses' father-in-law, Jethro, in Exodus 18:21. The people God wants in this river must be "able," meaning an army valiant, mighty, efficient, strong, forceful and powerful. These people must be "God-fearing," meaning those who revere and fear God and are terrified of operating outside His will. They must be people of "truth," meaning firm in their faith, sure, and reliable for the Lord. And they must have a "hatred for dishonest gain," for covetousness and for unjust profiteering. Where this river is going and where it needs to be going are two different directions. Are you willing and ready to jump into the river of politics and law to make a difference? God is looking for a few brave difference makers to enter these treacherous waters.

Hell or High Water

1. How has the enemy polluted this river?

Chris has described for you how the politics and law river's biblical origins go all the way back to Moses—the giver of the Law—and to Israel's judges, the keepers of it. After Moses and Joshua died, so did much of Israel's firsthand knowledge of God. The Israelites were constantly given over to sin, and were therefore given into the hands of their enemies. God intervened with judges: "Then the LORD raised up judges, who saved them out of the hands of these raiders" (Judges 2:16 NIV). So if everything was going so well—and it was—why did the Israelites get a king? In short, they just wanted to be like their neighboring nations who had kings. Didn't anybody stand up and remind them that they shouldn't covet their neighbors' kings? Yes, Samuel did. He warned the Israelites that kings can lay heavy burdens upon nations, and over time replace God as king. Not to mention that you never know if a king's sons will be worthy of inheritance. We even see an example of this in Numbers 27. After God used Moses to settle a dispute over daughters receiving inheritances when there were no sons, He then told Moses to let Joshua be his successor (rather than Moses' own sons). Some extrabiblical material called the Midrash (a thirteenth-century commentary written on these and other important passages) interjects here that on the heels of this inheritance dispute, Moses actually asked for his own sons to inherit his place over Israel, but God rejected the idea of a dynasty. That's where Numbers 27:22–23 (NIV) picks up, stating, "Moses did as the LORD commanded him. He took Joshua and had him stand before Eleazar the priest and the whole assembly. Then he laid his hands on him and commissioned him, as the LORD instructed through Moses." Whether or not you believe the Midrash is accurate, we must admit that it is consistent with God's view: *You don't need a monarchy. You need Me.*

2. How can God purify this river?

I give that historical detail here to make the point that many today do not believe it is even God's will for us to have a political river in the earth. If God were truly king, then why do we need kings or presidents or prime ministers? But the horse is already out of that gate, and we will likely never return to an era where Church and State are not separate. As such, we must learn to work with what the previous generations have handed to us and learn to purify this river of impact. Wherever you live, the politicians of your country make the laws that affect everything about your life, from the foods that are brought into your home, to the activities you are allowed to engage in, to the financial future of all of it. So it serves to reason that you need to be praying for these political and legal leaders. Also consider the fact that God may want you to become one of them. And no matter what post He leads you into, remember that at one time God favored judges over kings. Kings do not mingle amongst their people. Judges do. Kings are not intimately involved with the people of their community. Judges are. Simply put, God likes small government. So even if you make your way all the way to the highest banks of this river of politics and law, never forget that you work *for* the people, and that God is the King of all kings.

Head above Water—Doctor's Orders

1. What are my health risks in this river?

The American Bar Association released an online article entitled "New study on lawyer well-being reveals serious concerns for legal profession" that outlined two different studies exposing mental health disorders and substance abuse among law students and lawyers. Among the findings for law students were these statistics:

- 25 percent of law students are at risk for alcoholism.
- 17 percent of law students suffer from depression.
- 37 percent of law students report mild to severe anxiety.
- 6 percent of law students report having suicidal thoughts in the last year.[2]

And for practicing lawyers, the news was not much better:

- 28 percent of lawyers suffered from depression.
- 19 percent of lawyers had severe anxiety.
- 11.4 percent of lawyers had suicidal thoughts in the previous year.[3]

Statistics like these make you feel guilty about all those lawyer jokes you tell, right? No doubt it is a stressful industry, but politicians are just as at risk. And do you know why? Because the majority of politicians *are* lawyers! In fact, a 2020 article entitled, "Congress: Too Many Lawyers and Lifelong Politicians," states,

> Lawyer is the second most well-represented profession in Congress, with 157 members of the House identifying as attorneys. While there is one lawyer for every accountant in America, the ratio in Congress is more lopsided: 14 lawyers for every accountant.

This could explain why our tax code is 75,000 pages long and it still hasn't raised enough money to avoid $22 trillion in debt.[4]

And it isn't just the United States Congress that holds a high percentage of lawyers. American presidents also have a similar dubious distinction. We have had 46 presidencies at the time of this writing. That means there is the probability of those presidents having come from 45 different occupations. (Grover Cleveland was elected to two nonconsecutive terms, so he's considered the 22nd and 24th president.) But no . . . prior to coming to the White House, almost 60 percent of American presidents were—you guessed it—lawyers.

2. How can I protect myself in this river—body, mind and spirit?

The point of citing those statistics here is that if you are going to be in this politics and law river, you need to take extra measures to care for your health. You can do that in the following ways:

Physically: We just read some alarming statistics concerning alcoholism in this industry. If you are planning a career in this river, don't surround yourself with the temptations that have been proven to drown some of your colleagues. And these temptations will be everywhere—at every dinner and banquet as you rub elbows with the gatekeepers who can help advance your career. Set a new standard for yourself in front of them. Consider choosing a bottle of San Pelligrino—sparkling water—over wine. Adding lime will not only make it extra refreshing, but the vitamin C and antioxidants in the citrus are known to extend life. Refuse the booze, and blame it on medical science.

Emotionally: Make a note of those statistics about depression and anxiety. Lessen your chances of succumbing to these by surrounding yourself with positive people of faith. Show me your friends, and I will show you your future!

Spiritually: No job should drive you to suicide, yet we just read statistics that listed suicide as a danger in this river. Before you even dip one toe into this river, establish yourself spiritually. Ask yourself what kind of man or woman of God you want to be in ten years, and then be that person tomorrow. Find a church with praying people who will lift you up during trouble and calm you down during stress, and you will find that when you get to wherever you have set your political or legal sights, you will arrive there healthy—body, mind and spirit.

The Coast Is Clear

How can my spiritual personality make an impact in this river?

The apostle personality: If you have the apostle personality, you will either find yourself in a place, or wanting to get to a place, where you are in charge of people. You have the ability to lead, and your skills add excellence to every project you take on. A frontline position is just a few key stepping-stones away for you, and leadership has found you throughout your whole life and academic career. Whether it is on committees or in the courtroom, and whether you are a campaign manager or the candidate, your wisdom goes before you and your integrity has a long-lasting flavor in the fast-talking mouths of your judicial colleagues. Remember that you are the estuary that unites different streams of thought.

The prophet personality: If you have the prophet personality, you are a precise interpreter of the law. Like Moses and Deborah—who were both prophets and judges—you have a black-and-white perspective on political and judicial matters and a strong governing sense of right and wrong. As an underground river, you have the uncanny ability to deeply discern motives and are usually the first one in the room to perceive fraud and duplicity, which you are unafraid to confront. Leadership will find you, but until it does, be patient. Ask for God's timing on how to release what you discern so that it doesn't cost you a job that God has brought you as a stepping-stone to larger platforms. Sometimes, those with the prophet personality must hit their knees and pray.

The evangelist personality: If you have the evangelist personality, you had better like being on the front lines and at the center of political or judicial attention. How are you going to spend the favor of God that is on your life? You have the ability to communicate with precision and to rally people, which graces you with the enviable gift of winning others to your cause. Over the course of your career you will be given many podiums, some of which will present you with pulpit-like moments filled with purpose that bring you intense joy. Stay humble and God-focused every step along the way as you spread your whitewater rapids passion to the legal eagles and political pundits around you.

The pastor personality: If you have the pastor personality, you are in this river to serve, care for and defend the defenseless. Due to that, you stand out amongst your peers as being noticeably less competitive than they are, yet equally as driven. Your motivation is to benefit others. Whereas your colleagues are trying to get as far down the river as fast as they can, your pace is a little slower since your main concern is baptizing people in the gentle stream of God's love along the way. You are an advocate of the people. Even though you may have the charisma of a political candidate, you have the heart of the court reporter who is willing to present truth without recognition.

The teacher personality: If you have the teacher personality, the world is your classroom. There is not a single person along your path in this river that you do not want to share your insights with as he or she floats by, and yours are insights worth hearing! As a well-informed tributary of knowledge, you have an appreciation for history as it pertains to what it can show us about the future. There will be mentoring relationships aplenty, large and small, for you in this river. Seize the opportunities when you can since politicians and lawyers tend to be very transient people who are constantly climbing the ladder to their next level of conquest.

Walk on Water (from God's Word)

> May he also rule from sea to sea
> And from the River to the ends of the earth.
>
> Psalm 72:8

Military and Paramilitary River

Military Careers

Please note that the lists of military ranks (in ascending order of rank) are United States specific because these are the ones we as Americans are most familiar with. If you are from another country, think in terms of what the rankings would be in similar branches of your nation's military.

Air Force:

Airman basic

Airman

Airman first class

Senior airman

Staff sergeant

Technical sergeant

Master sergeant

Senior master sergeant

Chief master sergeant

Command chief master
sergeant

Chief master sergeant

Second lieutenant

First lieutenant

Captain

Major

Lieutenant colonel

Colonel

Brigadier general

Major general

Lieutenant general

General

Army:

Private

Private second class

Private first class

Specialist

Corporal

Sergeant

Staff sergeant

Sergeant first class

Master sergeant

First sergeant

Sergeant major

Command sergeant major

Sergeant major of the
Army

Second lieutenant

First lieutenant

Captain

Major

Lieutenant colonel

Colonel

Brigadier general

Major general

Lieutenant general

General

Coast Guard:

Seaman recruit

Seaman apprentice

Seaman

Petty officer third class

Petty officer second class

Petty officer first class

Chief petty officer

Senior chief petty officer

Master chief petty officer

Command master chief
petty officer

Master chief petty officer

Ensign

Lieutenant junior grade

Lieutenant

Lieutenant commander

Commander

Captain

Rear admiral lower half

Rear admiral

Vice admiral

Admiral

Marines:

Private

Private first class

Lance corporal

Corporal

Sergeant

Staff sergeant

Gunnery sergeant

Master sergeant

First sergeant

Master gunnery sergeant

Sergeant major

Second lieutenant

First lieutenant

Captain

Major

Lieutenant colonel

Colonel

Brigadier general

Major general

Lieutenant general

General

Navy:

Seaman recruit

Seaman apprentice

Seaman

Petty officer third class

Petty officer second class

Petty officer first class

Chief petty officer

Senior chief petty officer

Master chief petty officer

Command master CFO

Master chief petty officer

Ensign

Lieutenant junior grade

Lieutenant

Lieutenant commander

Commander

Captain

Rear admiral lower half

Rear admiral

Vice admiral

Admiral

Paramilitary Careers

Please note that the lists of paramilitary careers are also in order of ascending rank.

Local Police:

Police officer	Police captain
Police detective	Deputy chief
Police corporal	Assistant chief
Police sergeant	Chief of police
Police lieutenant	Police commissioner

County:

Bailiff	Captain
Deputy	Division chief
Corporal	
Sergeant	Assistant sheriff
Lieutenant	Sheriff

State Police:

Trooper	Major
Sergeant	Lieutenant colonel
Lieutenant	
Captain	Colonel

Federal (FBI):

Field agent	Special agent-in-charge
New agent trainee	FBI management
Special agent	Deputy assistant director
Senior special agent	Assistant director
Supervisory special agent	Associate executive assistant director
Assistant special agent-in-charge	Executive assistant director

Associate deputy director

Deputy chief of staff

Chief of staff

Special counsel to the
director

Deputy director

Director

Law Enforcement Variants:

Patrol officer

Detective

SWAT

Police dog (K-9) trainer

Police dog (K-9)

Bailiff

County detective

Game warden

Tribal officer

Indian agent

Lighthorse correction officer

Probation and parole officer

Park ranger

Federal air marshal

Marshal and deputy marshal

Special agent

Firefighters:

Volunteer firefighter

Inspector

Wildland firefighter

Firefighter engineer

Airport firefighter

Firefighter/EMT

Firefighter/paramedic

Fire investigator

Fire marshal

Fire chief

Come to the River

You, the military or paramilitary, come with a heart of courage and a will to defend and protect. God has uniquely fashioned and appointed you to resist evil. If you are military, you possess the courage to wage war in defense of sovereignty. If you are paramilitary, you possess the strength to guard and keep the peace. The fabric of your conscience is like armor, ready and willing to defend and uphold justice and order at a minute's notice. Fear is a foe, and terror your enemy. You understand the cost of life and are willing to lay yours down for the preservation of others. The world is a safer place because of you.

1. Where did this river start?

The earliest documented militia were Egyptian. This is not to say that wars were not waged in the world prior to the hieroglyphic era of Egyptian history. But it was the Egyptian rulers who were among the first to record images and produce relics that celebrated their victorious military campaigns, as early as 3200 BC under the reign of Scorpion I. Historically, the military and governance worked hand in hand. To establish a dynasty or kingdom, rulers needed the ability to defend their existing assets, while boasting a means for acquiring future assets. The military was synonymous with empire. The most prized asset in the early periods of civilization was the region of the Tigris-Euphrates river system known as Mesopotamia, now modern-day Turkey, Syria and Iraq. These famous Garden of Eden waters, stretching from the mountain regions of southeastern Turkey to the Persian Gulf, were as valuable for economic superiority in the region as the oil reserves of the Middle East are today. Names like Darius, Xerxes, Alexander the Great, Ptolemy and King Daruis III all fought to control the "Fertile Crescent" region of Northern Mesopotamia. The Egyptian, Babylonian, Persian, Greek and Roman empires waged war for control of these waterways for transportation, irrigation and export. Without a strong military, an empire was just one defeat away from losing everything. But with a strong military and paramilitary, a nation could sustain itself for centuries.

2. Where is this river going?

Has this really changed? As long as there are humans, there will be conquests. The fallen nature of mankind demands power, recognition and fame. So regardless of how progressive and modern we become, there will always be a need for those who are charged to protect, defend and keep the peace. The news media is overrun with images of war and stories of increased lawlessness in our cities. As these events unfold, just as Jesus forewarned us that they would, our military and paramilitary personnel must be ready and prepared to defend and protect the rights, welfare and lives of the innocent. As this spirit of lawlessness increases, our local and state police, our sheriffs and border patrol agents, our first responders and marshals, will need to be prepared to protect those who might fall victim to this lawless agenda. Just as Jesus told His disciples to sell their garments and buy a sword (as a means of protection, not aggression; see Luke 22:35–38), our military and paramilitary river personnel must be prepared to defend and protect those in their care and endure against this destructive wave of assault coming against our culture. In Psalm 121, God is described as Jehovah Shamar—a keeper, a protector and a guard.[1] As a God-appointed military and paramilitary member, you are to carry His heart of protection and peacekeeping into the world. Rise up and be blessed, you who enforce peace, for you shall be called sons of God! (see Matthew 5:9).

Hell or High Water

1. How has the enemy polluted this river?

As Chris said, history shows that nations have always used their militaries to establish their kingdoms, defend their assets and increase them. It is the "increasing your assets" part that can get a nation in trouble if there is greed involved. How much land does one person need? How much power must one nation exercise over another? Why do the nations rage? Jesus told us very bluntly that this would happen in the last days. Listen to His words in the special promise at the end of Matthew 24:6–13:

> You will be hearing of wars and rumors of wars. See that you are not frightened, for those things must take place, but that is not yet the end. For nation will rise against nation, and kingdom against kingdom, and in various places there will be famines and earthquakes. But all these things are merely the beginning of birth pangs.
>
> Then they will deliver you to tribulation, and will kill you, and you will be hated by all nations because of My name. At that time many will fall away and will betray one another and hate one another. Many false prophets will arise and will mislead many. Because lawlessness is increased, most people's love will grow cold. But the one who endures to the end, he will be saved.

2. How can God purify this river?

Look at the nation of Israel as an example of what pure motives are in war. Its military exists to defend its assets, but has never been interested in increasing them. It wants to defend the boundaries of the Promised Land assigned to it, but you never hear of Israel venturing out to conquer other countries around the world to expand its boundaries. And as I established in my "MapQuest" section in chapter 3, when Noah's Ark came to rest on Mount Ararat his three sons populated the entire earth, so you are related to one of them! But it was only Shem who stayed put and didn't venture out, as his brothers did, to populate the rest of the world. Shem stayed put to become the father of the Semite people. He merely wanted to defend what God has said was theirs. Moses came along about four hundred years later and officially led the Israelites out of captivity. Entering their Promised Land involved defeating the Philistine ("Palestine") giants in the land, and that is why today the Palestinians think they are the ones who have been encroached upon. In truth, from the moment Noah and his family stepped out of the Ark and into a promise of their new world, God knew that the Promised Land would belong to the Israelites. I like to think of that Flood as the rushing river that baptized the whole world with a fresh start. For our militaries to maintain God's perspective and success, they will have to rid themselves of all greed and take a lesson from the army of God's chosen people, Israel.

Head above Water—Doctor's Orders

1. What are my health risks in this river?

Let's start with the military and statistics about being in the Armed Forces: A 2022 article from the Army Public Health Center (APHC) states,

> Musculoskeletal injuries caused by acute (sudden) incidents as well as chronic repeated stresses to the body (overuse), have been described as the single biggest health problem of the U.S. Military because:

- Almost 50% of military experience 1 or more injury each year.
- They result in over 2,000,000 medical encounters annually across military Services.
- They require 90–120 or more days of restricted work or lost duty time, in addition to the cost of treatment.
- Most are overuse strains, sprains, and stress fractures; most to lower extremities (ankle/foot, knee/lower leg).
- More than half of these injuries are exercise or sports-related, especially running.
- Back and shoulder injuries are also common, more often associated with lifting and carrying activities.[2]

As for the paramilitary, listen to these statistics the National Library of Medicine published in a study of injuries among law enforcement and other paramilitary:

Methods: We characterized injuries among emergency medical services (EMS), firefighting, and police occupations by using data from the National Electronic Injury Surveillance System Occupational Supplement (NEISS-Work) for injuries treated in US hospital emergency departments in 2000–2001.

Results: Sprains and strains were the leading injury (33–41%) among EMS, firefighter, and police occupations. Police officers and career firefighters had the highest injury rates (8.5 and 7.4 injuries per 100 full-time equivalent workers, respectively).

Conclusions: The physical demands of emergency response are a leading cause of injuries that may benefit from similar interventions across the occupations.[3]

2. How can I protect myself in this river—body, mind and spirit?

Physically: The previous APHC study plainly goes on to state that not all injuries can be avoided, but that unit leaders should strive to reduce injuries and increase prevention by taking into account environmental factors such as rugged terrain or extreme weather.

Emotionally: Alarmingly, on the National Center for PTSD's homepage at the U.S. Department of Veteran Affairs, the opening words admit,

> When you serve in the military you may be exposed to different types of traumas than civilians. The war you served in may also affect your risk because of the types of trauma that were common. War zone deployment, training accidents and military sexual trauma (or, MST) may lead to PTSD.[4]

The page went on to list PTSD risks by service era, and the statistics go as high as 20 percent for the development of PTSD postwar. I have members of every armed service branch in my family. When one of them returned from an overseas deployment with a severe case of PTSD, that was part of my motivation to invent my essential oil blend, Quiet Brain, which this family member said "turned off" the PTSD. It was testimonies like this, and many more, that caused us to secure a U.S. patent for this oil blend as a "Neurological Composition," even though only 5 percent of natural products get patented. (I highly recommend Quiet Brain if you struggle with PTSD, anxiety, migraine, or any other neurological issue. You can learn more about Quiet Brain by visiting NeuromaticsOil.com.)

Spiritually: Whether you are military or paramilitary, behind a desk or on the front lines, remember that you serve a country that declares itself to be "One nation under God." Put Him first in everything you do, and rise to the top of the ranks as your obedience to Him attracts His favor on your career.

The Coast Is Clear

How can my spiritual personality make an impact in this river?

The apostle personality: If you have the apostle personality, the duties of commissioning find you often. You will wind up in top-ranking roles because of your ability to remain level-headed while you troubleshoot and bring wisdom during emergencies. Although you have been in the field and have paid your dues there, your top-level authority as an estuary in this river is to bring all teams and streams together to get the job done. You have the respect of those you lead, but remember to maintain their trust by remaining a person of integrity, both in public and private.

The prophet personality: If you have the prophet personality, you are justice driven and ready to take on any enemy. You are fearless and do not shy away from confrontation. Your patriotism runs deep, because remember, you are the underground river that is willing to be covert in order to avoid compromise. Do not become impatient during hidden seasons. Like any underground water supply, you will arise ready for the challenge at a moment's notice and spring into action. Always be willing to edify, exhort and comfort those around you, while remembering that you may be the one who discerns trouble coming a mile away.

The evangelist personality: If you have the evangelist personality, God has graced you to rally a crowd and proclaim the way forward. Whether in the military, law enforcement or behind the scenes, you will be very helpful in group projects and events that require rallying. You are always in the thick of things, giving directions and helping put out proverbial fires with your whitewater rapids ideas. The favor of God on your life makes you an excellent candidate for giving directives that seem both appealing and attainable to everyone around you, so remain confident in expressing them. Communication is your middle name.

The pastor personality: If you have the pastor personality, then you bring love and peace to this river of warriors. You are the gentle stream that flows through every conversation and emergency situation you find yourself in. You take seriously your commitment to protect and defend others, not because you signed on the dotted line, but because your heart is hardwired to do so. You are the helping hands in a room full of boots and badges. Despite the number of stripes on your sleeve, stars on your shoulders, K-9s under your care or SWAT team members on your team, people will value your compassionate counsel and seek you out for it.

The teacher personality: If you have the teacher personality, you will ultimately find yourself in a position of training many others. Like the tributary that branches off into many flowing directions at once, you are a great multitasker who helps keep the team informed. You see inefficiencies and can bring instruction, training and guidance into the problem, getting everybody on the same page. Your self-discipline is contagious, and you are a natural-born coach or commander. Remember that just as important as knowing the right thing to do is knowing God's timing on when to do it.

Walk on Water (from God's Word)

> And the LORD will utterly destroy
> The tongue of the Sea of Egypt;
> And He will wave His hand over the River
> With His scorching wind;
> And He will strike it into seven streams
> And make men walk over dry-shod.
>
> Isaiah 11:15

16

Creativity River (Fine Arts and Intellectual Property)

Creativity industry (fine arts and intellectual property) careers include (but are not limited to) these:

3-D product design	Authors
Advertising agents	Book cover designers
Airbrush artists	Book publishing
Animators	Book storyboard illustrators
Architects	Cake decorators
Art gallery curators	Cartoonists
Art historians	Ceramics artists
Art therapists	Chefs
Artists	Children's book illustrators

Choreographers
Comic book illustrators
Composers
Concept artists
Craft designers
Digital artists
Directors of photography
Engineers
Event planners
Fashion designers
Fashion illustrators
Fashion photographers
Film storyboard illustrators
Floral designers
Foley artists
Font designers
Food photographers
Glaziers
Grant writers
Graphic designers
Greeting card creators
Illustrators
Interior designers
Jewelers
Landscape architects
Lighting designers
Literary agents
Logo/branding designers
Lyricists
Magazine and periodical
  publishing

Magazine layout designers
Makeup artists
Marketing directors
Music photographers
Musicians
Painters
Personal stylists
Photojournalists
Portrait photographers
Potter/ceramic designers
Research and development
  (R&D)
Screenwriters
Sculptors
Seamstress/wardrobe designers
Set/stage designers
Stained-glass window designers
Tattoo artists
Technical writers
Telecopy (TV) writers
Textile worker/artists
Toys and games developers
Travel photographers
Typographers
Video editors
Video game designers
Weavers
Web designers
Wedding photographers
Wildlife photographers
Wood-carvers

Come to the River

You who bring beauty and color to our senses through words, images, sounds, objects and flavors, thank you! You carry the creative imagination of God. Your world is a world of inspiration. You see each day not for what it is, but for what it could be. You feel a sense of responsibility to create because you are convinced that the fruits of your labors contain the very substances that will heal, satisfy, awaken and affirm the very heart and soul of humanity. And, like a proud new parent, you can't wait to show off the fruits of your labors.

1. Where did this river start?

Bezalel and Oholiab are names that most people are unfamiliar with in biblical history. Let's read their story out of Exodus 31:1–11:

> Now the LORD spoke to Moses, saying, "See, I have called by name Bezalel, the son of Uri, the son of Hur, of the tribe of Judah. I have filled him with the Spirit of God in wisdom, in understanding, in knowledge, and in all kinds of craftsmanship, to make artistic designs for work in gold, in silver, and in bronze, and in the cutting of stones for settings, and in the carving of wood, that he may work in all kinds of craftsmanship. And behold, I Myself have appointed with him Oholiab, the son of Ahisamach, of the tribe of Dan; and in the hearts of all who are skillful I have put skill, that they may make all that I have commanded you: the tent of meeting, and the ark of testimony, and the mercy seat upon it, and all the furniture of the tent, the table also and its utensils, and the pure gold lampstand with all its utensils, and the altar of incense, the altar of burnt offering also with all its utensils, and the laver and its stand, the woven garments as well, and the holy garments for Aaron the priest, and the garments of his sons, with which to carry on their priesthood; the anointing oil also, and the fragrant incense for the holy place, they are to make them according to all that I have commanded you."

This is the birthplace of fine arts in the earth!

2. Where is this river going?

Creative people hear silent words, imagine what cannot be touched, and see what could become. Then they devote themselves to the self-sacrificing process of making all of this tangible for the world to enjoy. I know this river well. It's the river I look forward to jumping into more than any other. This river is flowing with an ability to influence like no other. It is an advertising jingle or slogan, a song, a book, a movie script, a social media post, and even that recipe everyone is taking about. This river is designed to stir people on an emotional level. The abilities of the Renaissance artists caused a "rebirth" in civilization spiritually, economically and politically. Because of its powerful influence, creativity must be handled with care, integrity and humility. It is a God-given ability that He intends to be used for good, so don't allow it to be misused for evil.

Hell or High Water

1. How has the enemy polluted this river?

You would think that since the Creator is the source of all creation and all things creative, He would have total control over the creativity that flows to-and-fro across the earth. But like everything else that was set up on the precept of humanity's free will, we have not all stewarded the Creator's gift of creativity with pure hearts. You see it today in everything from secular ads online to secular television commercials. Alongside whatever is being advertised to you, there is an ungodly undercurrent pushing its agenda on you. It tries to convince you that a small demographic of wickedness is the accepted status quo. The media has normalized sin. Eniola Alabi, in her book *Racially Influenced Witchcraft: A Biblical Perspective*, comments on this. And please note the thoughts she includes from internationally influential author and pastor Francis Frangipane:

> Apart from using dreams, visions, imaginations, texts and words sent directly to people, there could also be demonic and satanic control using the media as it communicates to people. *The negative*

situations mentioned in the earlier paragraph could also be sown this way. The enemy could use this avenue to misinform, sow strife, confusion and division among people. This method is also used to mislead and to misguide. The enemy usually employs this method when targeting several individuals or groups of people.

Pastor Francis Frangipane, in his book 'The Three Battlegrounds,' wrote:

And the serpent poured water like a river out of his mouth after the woman, so that he might cause her (**the church**) to be swept away with the flood. (**Revelation 12:15**)

Water, in this context, symbolizes 'words'. In our world there exists a flood of **words** and **visual images** coming out of the mouth of Satan. . . .

In our information-filled, entertainment-oriented world, even minor demons can exercise major influence simply by possessing the script writers and producers of movies and television . . .

So Satanic images and communications are some ways in which the enemy tries to exercise satanic control and influence.

Witchcraft control seeks to mislead and to misguide and to try to bring about, in the life of the person that is being attacked, situations that are not according to God's purpose . . .

Some level of witchcraft control is involved in the manipulation of the media by some people seeking to demoralise those with whom they have disagreement.[1]

We could also quote the same text in our next chapter, which talks about the entertainment and recreation river. Yet I believe that in the quote within the quote from Frangipane above, he is addressing those in this chapter's creativity river—the behind-the-scenes writers and creators of words and images that will eventually fill the mouths of the entertainers we will address in the chapter ahead.

2. How can God purify this river?

Remember that there is not an increase in demons on the earth today, even though the increase in evil would make it seem as though there is. And remember that only a third of the angels fell from heaven and that the remaining heavenly angels still outnumber them 2 to 1. Demons do not procreate and give birth to baby demons, so we still have the majority advantage with our angelic protection! But just one Hollywood writer with a minor demonic influence can use his or her platform to give the impression of having major demonic influence in the world.

So let's flip that around: If you are a creator out there—whatever your creative medium or genre—use your gifts to create art and content that have majority impact on culture! That is how you purify this vital river of impact in the earth today.

Head above Water—Doctor's Orders

1. What are my health risks in this river?

In this river you can encounter a myriad of potential health risks, and in a moment I will itemize some of them, with their methods of protection. But I want to discuss one risk that unfortunately transcends every career path and industry in this sector, and that is the risk of isolation, which leads to mental illness. The reason this risk transcends the others is because many people in this category are entrepreneurs who often find themselves working alone. Either that, or they have been entrusted with the ability to work from home by their employer or contracted agent. If you are in this category, you may spend a great deal of time by yourself. While this is sometimes good for the creative process, too much isolation can lead to depression and more. A VeryWellMind.com article entitled "The Link Between Depression and Creativity" states,

> The notion that depression and other forms of mental illness go hand-in-hand with creativity is so prevalent that it gave rise to the terms "tortured artist" and "mad artist." But is this idea just a stereotype, or does it actually contain a grain of truth?
>
> Painters such as Vincent van Gogh, who famously cut off his ear and ultimately took his life in 1890, contribute to this idea,

as does the writer Sylvia Plath, who died by suicide in 1963. Both artists detailed their mental illness in writing.

Van Gogh sent an 1888 letter to his brother Theo explaining, "I am unable to describe exactly what is the matter with me. Now and then there are horrible fits of anxiety, apparently without cause, or otherwise a feeling of emptiness and fatigue in the head . . . at times I have attacks of melancholy and of atrocious remorse."[2]

2. How can I protect myself in this river—body, mind and spirit?

Physically: Those who spend long days under a laptop need a radiation resistant pad, such as the HARApad I mentioned in chapter 12, which I have used for years. If you are an artist who works with various textiles, pigments and metals, make sure you are minimizing your exposure to heavy-metal poisoning and harmful dyes, and always wear the necessary protective gear to prevent toxicity. If you are a glazier, be careful to follow all safety protocols for installing glass when at high altitudes.

Emotionally: Avoid extended periods of isolation. Surround yourself with Christians who cheer you on in your creative process, yet who also come knock on your door when they think the solitude is getting the best of you.

Spiritually: Let's pray for a renaissance revival of the Bezalel and Oholiab anointing. Create under the inspiration of the Holy Spirit! And if you are an entrepreneur or work in a freelance capacity, take a vow of integrity so that you might do your work with excellence and have maximum cultural impact. Your creations are the lifeblood of the creative economy! Your words, floral decorations, tile work, music, sculptures, stained glass, videos, interior design, dances, metalwork, makeup artistry, pottery, graphic designs, tapestries, mosaics, foods and photographs paint God's earthly world with heaven's color. Always stay close to Him, for your creativity flows directly from the Creator Himself.

The Coast Is Clear

How can my spiritual personality make an impact in this river?

The apostle personality: If you have the apostle personality, you have the potential to be a creative entrepreneur in this global sector. Though you are a highly creative person in your own right, your ability to lead others and to streamline their sometimes disorganized ideas into one current only underscores your role as an estuary in this industry. When you see creative potential in others, you encourage them and call it out, while providing places for them to flow in their gifts. Because of that, creatives see you as a trusted confidant and sounding board for their budding innovations.

The prophet personality: If you have the prophet personality, you are the one whom the apostle personality has been praying for in his or her business! You are an idea factory, and producing creative content is as easy as breathing for you. With more hours in the day, you might actually remember sleeping and eating and other important self-care priorities. But for you, self-care is secondary to creating. You are a deep and constantly flowing underwater river of inspiration. So remember that your words, images and creations in their various forms will do much more than entertain the world. They have the potential to change it.

The evangelist personality: If you have the evangelist personality, you have the revelation that your creations and innovations have the potential to bear fruit that is eternal, not just temporal. Whether you dance, draw or determine the direction for advertising campaigns, your message always rises to the top and is your number one mission. Your life is a creative crusade, and the world is watching. You have the gift of creative persuasion and must remember to let your whitewater rapid convictions influence your industry and neutralize the enemy's agenda that is flowing through it. Fast-moving water is the cleanest.

The pastor personality: If you have the pastor personality, you don't create for the sake of creating, but for the sake of helping others. With every design, production and concept you birth, you see faces along the way of people who need its truths, and you create with them in mind. A gentle stream, you are willing to be in the spotlight but don't have to be, which sets you apart from the other personalities in this creative industry. The thought of something you wrote, designed, filmed, painted, cooked or edited bringing someone encouragement and direction makes you feel purposeful despite the paycheck, which you will gladly sacrifice if the project calls for it.

The teacher personality: If you have the teacher personality, you are not only always ready to bring a creative teaching, but you also have good friends who can film, chop and score it to turn it into something compelling. In fact, you might even be able to do all of the above yourself. You are able to create visual aids—with objects or words—that reach a variety of hearts and minds. You usually have several project ideas rushing through your head at the same time, because remember, you are the tributary. You stand out among your peers as being both creative and administrative—left brain and right brain—and it causes you to be a highly productive innovator.

Walk on Water (from God's Word)

Now on the last day, the great day of the feast, Jesus stood and cried out, saying, "If anyone is thirsty, let him come to Me and drink. He who believes in Me, as the Scripture said, 'From his innermost being will flow rivers of living water.'"

John 7:37–38

Entertainment and Recreation River

Entertainment and recreation industry careers include (but are not limited to) these:

Entertainment Industry:

Audio production studios

Film animation services

Film industry

Home shopping TV

Independent music labels

Literary agencies

Major label music production

Modeling agencies

Motion picture film processing

Movie and video distribution

Movie and video
   production
Movie theatres
Music publishing
Musical groups and artists
Public relations
Radio broadcasting
Talent agencies

Talent and literary agencies
Television broadcasting
Television production
Publishing
Video games
Video postproduction
   services

Connecting Careers:

Actors
Audio engineers
Boom operators
Broadcast designers
Broadcasters
Broadway promoters
Cinematographers
Dancers
Disc jockeys
Editors
Executive producers
Fashion editors
Film directors
Film editors
Film producers
Foley artists
Home shopping hosts
Journalists
Line producers
Livestreamers
Marketing directors

Masters of ceremonies
Media consultants
Media planning
Media proprietors
Music editors (filmmaking)
NBC pages
News analysts
News presenters
News producers
Panel operators
Performing artists
Playwrights
Poster artists
Production company
Production team
Property masters
Publicists
Screenwriters
Script coordinators
Script editors
Showrunners

Special effects supervisors
Spotlight operators
Stage management
Stereographers
Technical communication
Technical crew
Technicians
Television program creators

Theatre practitioners
Unit still photographers
VFX creative directors
Video editors
Visual effects supervisors
Wardrobe supervisors
Weather reporters/
  presenters

Recreation:

Amusement parks
Arcades
Bowling centers
Celebrity and sports agents
Concert and event
  promotion
Family fun centers
Golf courses and country
  clubs
Golf driving ranges
Fantasy sports services
Historic sites
Marinas
MLB athletes and franchise
MLS athletes and franchise

Museums
National parks
Nature institutions
NBS athletes and franchise
NFL athletes and franchise
NHL athletes and franchise
Racing and individual
  sports
Ski and snowboard resorts
Sports franchises
USFL athletes and franchise
WNBA athletes and
  franchise
WWE wrestlers and
  franchise

Come to the River

You who desire or have been given the platform, the stage, the screen or the field, or if you work closely with others who appear on them, you have the public's attention. You have found (or will find) yourself in this place through hard work, dedication, favor and talent. Your popularity will be enriching, yet it will come with a high price. Your life is not your own. You are flowing in a public river. All eyes are on you. It appears from the riverbanks to be all fun and games, but you will find that there are things hiding in these waters that will require caution and self-control. Are you ready to entertain us?

1. Where did this river start?

Merriam-Webster defines entertainment as "amusement or diversion," and "something diverting or engaging."[1] It has been medicine for the world throughout history. King Solomon's vulnerable confession of his attempts to try to "amuse" the deepest needs of his soul with a variety of pleasures, including wine, success, homes, gardens, parks, ponds, fruit trees, slaves, owning flocks, possessing gold and silver, and providing himself with male and female singers and concubines, ended with his famous observation that it was all vanity and striving after the wind (see Ecclesiastes 2:1–11). Throughout history, people have been trying to find a diversion, a reason to laugh, an escape, a way to distract themselves from the complexities of life. It is the same today. The entertainment industry has evolved from the satirical plays and love stories that have come down to us from Menander (342–291 BC), to Shakespeare (AD 1564–1616), to Mozart (AD 1756–1791), to the silent movies of Charlie Chaplin in the early 1900s, to the social media celebrities of today. We look to entertainers to help us forget how hard life can be, but too much of a good thing is not always the best medicine for the doctor or the patient.

2. Where is this river going?

As our world becomes more closely connected through the Internet, and as we allow more and more digital distribution channels to populate our smartphones and cable servers, the world will continue to find itself in an entertainment candy store . . . or drugstore. Content of all kinds is just a touch away 24/7. People's insatiable demand for entertainment will continue to fuel a need for entertainment companies and entertainers. Whether your office is a ball field, an ice rink, a stage or a screen, the world just can't get enough. And until we get to the place that King Solomon got to, the opportunities will just keep coming. Entertainment companies and entertainers will have to ask the question, *What am I feeding the world? Do I want my entertainment talents to offer a momentary reprieve from the complexities of life, or am I wanting to become the focus of the world's attention?* It has been my personal experience in this industry that those who keep a healthy, God-fearing perspective on their talent in this highly impressionable industry have the greatest opportunity to provide a reprieve, and they will not be held responsible for feeding the addiction.

Hell or High Water

1. How has the enemy polluted this river?

The enemy has not only polluted this river, but has polluted many of those within it. One major way has been through addiction. Sometimes I wonder if the river of entertainment and recreation is filled with booze between its banks and not water at all. Think of all the Hollywood celebrities and sports stars who have drowned in this river! The American Addiction Centers released a recent article entitled "The Entertainment Industry and Addiction in America," which states this about the glamorization of alcohol and drugs:

> The acceptance of substance abuse has spilled over from the entertainment world, where addiction is not only displayed but all too often glamorized. Myths about addiction are spread by celebrities and overblown in the popular media. Television shows and movies contain appreciable amounts of substance abuse, and drug and alcohol use are common themes throughout all genres of music. Some concerning findings regarding the barrage of substance use throughout the entertainment world include:
>
> • Drugs are present in nearly half of all music videos, including alcohol (35%), tobacco (10%), and illicit drugs (13%).
> • 1 drinking scene is shown on television every 22 minutes, 1 smoking scene every 57 minutes, and 1 illicit drug use scene every 112 minutes.

- 71% of prime-time television programs depict alcohol use, 19% depict tobacco use, 20% mention illicit drug use, and 3% depict illicit drug use.
- More than 1/3 of all drinking scenes on television shows are humorous, while less than 1/4 of drinking scenes show any negative consequences.
- The average teenager is exposed to nearly 85 drug references a day in popular music.
- 40% of profiles on social networking websites reference substance abuse.[2]

2. How can God purify this river?

If we are going by my previous analogy of this industry's riverbanks overflowing with booze, then we need the river drained and refilled with God's living water. I know it seems impossible to imagine this industry without the presence of alcohol—*and drugs*—but the tide seems to be turning in favor of abstinence. I was excited to read a recent *Harper's Bazaar* article entitled "55 Celebrities Who Don't Drink Alcohol."[3] The article reported that superstars like Natalie Portman, Shania Twain, Tyler, The Creator, Blake Lively, Tyra Banks, Dane Cook, and Jennifer Lopez say they choose not to drink at all. Actress/singer Jennifer Hudson and director/actress Gillian Jacobs say they have never had a drink in their lives. Others like British tennis star Andy Murray admit that they now refrain from drinking after coming through severe addiction, which is also the testimony of actors Jim Carrey, Bradley Cooper, Rob Lowe, Samuel L. Jackson, Matthew Perry and Brad Pitt, as well as singers such as Keith Urban and Coldplay's Chris Martin. And as for us—Chris and Laura Smith—we are definitely in a convergence of the creativity river from chapter 16 and this entertainment river (not to mention the ministry river from chapter 22), so we made a decision almost forty years ago that we would choose a lifestyle of total abstinence from alcohol. Back then, in the first year of our marriage, we decided that rather than flirting with the danger lurking in every creative corner and at every industry banquet, we would make this small sacrifice, which has turned out to have such a big impact. We have never regretted it once.

Head above Water—Doctor's Orders

1. What are my health risks in this river?

We have focused a lot on entertainment industry perils, so let's now look at the recreation industry filled with athletes. A Health-Day article entitled "Professional Athletes" cites these alarming statistics:

> Professional athletes risk injury every time they train, practice, and compete. It's not surprising, then, that professional athletes were among five occupations that had more than 1,000 injuries per 10,000 workers. Athletes and sports competitors suffer more than 2,000 injuries per 10,000 workers, according to the Bureau of Labor Statistics. (Only an athlete, for example, is likely to experience turf toe, pitcher's elbow, or a sports hernia.) Getting hurt is a part of sports, but today's injuries play a larger role—and receive more attention from teams and the media alike—than at any time in sports history.
>
> The 2000s saw injuries increase in three major U.S. sports: the National Football League (NFL), major league baseball, and the National Hockey League. [4]

The article goes on to say this about concussions:

> Officials are also strictly enforcing rule changes prohibiting helmet-to-helmet contact and striking an opponent above the shoulders. Stiff penalties, fines, and suspensions accompany violations of these rules. Still, concussions remain a problem, possibly because today's athletes are bigger, faster, and stronger than in previous years. [5]

Let's look more at how athletes and actors and everyone in between can protect themselves from the risks that are a major part of this river.

181

2. How can I protect myself in this river—body, mind and spirit?

Physically: If you are a professional athlete, never be afraid to ask for the correct protective gear, and remember to protect your skull at all costs! Also, whether you are in the sports or recreation arenas, set an example of self-control and abstinence not only in your personal life, but also in the professional projects and events you participate in. In fact, whatever river you are in, *please* let the next book on your reading list be a free resource I wrote on the science, Scriptures and statistics on this topic of alcohol. It's called *Wine and Spirits*, and you can download it for free right now at www.lauraharrissmith.com/ebooks.

Emotionally: If you are setting your sights on fame or on being in an industry of famous people, remember this dictionary definition of celebrity: "the state of being celebrated."[6] Decide early on that you will not participate in celebrity worship, which is, of course, idolatry. Celebrate and worship Christ alone, and never enthrone anything or anyone else in your thoughts or affections (not even yourself).

Spiritually: Surround yourself with godly men and women who speak truth to you. You will need to be in close and regular contact with these mentors, pastors, parents or spiritual parents, and with those who will pray for you and speak wisdom to you whether you like it or not. Find a local church and make it part of your weekly life to attend and serve there. No one is exempt from this need in their lives. Never swim naked in this river, meaning keep yourself covered in pastoral prayer! Spiritual skinny-dipping will just leave you as a quotable statistic for history to mourn.

The Coast Is Clear

How can my spiritual personality make an impact in this river?

The apostle personality: If you have the apostle personality, your sights are set on the top, or should be. Once there (or if you are already there) you will carry a tremendous amount of responsibility. Your decision-making and directing skills have the potential to impact millions. Whether you are a line producer, a lineman coach, or a league franchise CEO, you are the estuary that brings many talents together for a successful outcome. Be sober about the level of influence and authority you have with the masses, and remember always to speak into the lives of those you lead. You may just be the only spiritual father or spiritual mother they have.

The prophet personality: If you have the prophet personality, you are a good judge of character and will be able to quickly discern a lack of honesty and integrity in these waters. Your first assignment as an underground river will always be to pray, but eventually you will come up for air and speak truth to many— and not just to your colleagues, but to the masses whom you all influence. You must keep your guard up and trust your spiritual sensitivity and intuition, since you constantly will be faced with temptations to compromise. You are the pure voice in a river full of many false prophets.

The evangelist personality: If you have the evangelist personality, you are someone who excels at rallying others, and who can persuade many to attend the shows, games and events you will inevitably find yourself a part of. You have the skills to serve as a propagator, which is a person who promotes an idea or theory. In this industry, a propagator can find success in marketing and publicity, and in spokesperson roles. Your whitewater rapid convictions will cleanse this river and allow you to rescue many who are drowning in it. You have the ability to be center stage or backstage, but you will not stay behind the scenes for very long.

The pastor personality: If you have the pastor personality, you are the gentle stream in this river of hard-driven ambition. You are the quiet heart in this river full of loudmouths. You will always be the first one to see those who are going under, and you will have the right words that throw them a line. They will seek you out for trustworthy counsel, even though the transient nature of this industry means that they may not stay in your life for long. Your humility is the elixir that prevents their pride and ego from manifesting in each conversation,

183

so never underestimate the power of the meekness you naturally possess. Remember Proverbs 15:1: "A gentle answer turns away wrath."

The teacher personality: If you have the teacher personality, you and your teams will use your communication abilities to reach and teach the world. You desire to use your platform for instruction, and the opportunities will be endless to do so. Choose wisely, since no tributary can be spread too thin. From film sets to ball fields to fashion runways, you are able to represent truth and set a standard with your training, directing, promoting, broadcasting and coaching. You are a constant flow of information and are the MVP whom many will thank. When your efforts go unseen, remember that the One who gave you your gifts is pleased.

Walk on Water (from God's Word)

> The lotus plants cover him with shade;
> The willows of the brook surround him.
> If a river rages, he is not alarmed;
> He is confident, though the Jordan rushes to his mouth.
>
> Job 40:22–23

Consumer Services and Commerce River

Consumer services and commerce industry careers include (but are not limited to) these:

Accidental death and dis-memberment (AD&D) insurance

Accounting

Agricultural industry

Air traffic control

Aircraft rental services

Airline catering services

Airline industry

Armored transportation services

Audio and visual equipment rental

Audit services

Auto extended warranty providers

Auto leasing, loans and sales financing

Automobile insurance

Banking

Batting cages

Beauty, spa and salon

Biotechnology consultants

Boat rentals

Bond management

Business brokers

Business insurance

Carpenters

Cash register services

Catering

Check cashing services

Commercial aircraft
leasing

Commercial auto insurance

Commercial banking

Commercial construction
insurance

Commodity dealing and
brokerage

Company research services

Construction machinery
rentals

Construction management

Construction workers

Contractors' insurance

Credit card issuing

Credit card processing and
money transferring

Credit repair services

Credit unions

Custody, asset and securities
services

Cyber liability insurance

Data center colocation
services

Daycare

Dental insurance

Detectives

Disability insurance

Distribution and logistics
consulting services

E-commerce

E-discovery consulting
services

E-discovery software
publishing

E-trading software
developers

Education consultants

Electricians

Employee assistance program
services

Entertainment insurance

Entrepreneurs

Finance and insurance

Financial data service
providers

Financial planning and
advice

Fire insurance

Food and beverage

Food delivery

Foreign currency exchange services

Forensic accounting services

Foster care

Franchise resale brokers and consultants

Group purchasing organizations

Handyman

Health and medical insurance

Health and welfare funds

Hedge funds

High frequency trading

Home warranty providers

Homeowners' insurance

Hospitality industry

Hotel/lodging

Housekeeping

Human resource managers

Human resources

HVAC services

Identity theft insurance

Industrial banks

Installers

Installment lenders

Insurance brokers and agencies

Insurance claims processing software

International trade financing

Investment banking and securities dealing

Landscapers

Leasing industry

Life insurance and annuities

Loan administration

Loan brokers

Long-term care insurance

Marketing consultants

Merchant banking services

Money transferring services

Mortgage refinancing providers

Mortgage title services

Mutual fund management

Online insurance brokers

Online stores

Open-end investment funds

Organic crop farming

Organic milk production

Pawn shops

Payday loan services

Pension fund management

Personal finance and money management

Pizza delivery services

Plumbers

Portfolio management

Prepaid credit and debit card providers

Private banking services

Private equity, hedge funds and investments

Product returns management services

Product warranty insurance

Property, casualty and direct insurance

Real estate

Real estate investment trusts

Real estate loans and collateralized debt

Regional banks

Reinsurance carriers

Rental property

Renters' insurance

Repairperson

Restaurants

Retail stores

Retirement and pension plans

Reverse mortgages providers

Sanitation

Savings banks and thrifts

Securities brokering

Security systems

Social work

Stock and commodity exchanges

Stock price and rating research

Subprime auto loans

Supply chain management services

Taxi services

Third-party administrators and insurance claims adjusters

Title insurance

Tourism

Transportation

Travel insurance

Trucking

Trusts and estates

Typing services

Venture capital and principal trading

Vision insurance

Weather forecasting services

Wholesale trade

Workers' compensation insurance

Come to the River

You who have entrepreneurial, business and/or administrative gifts that can be used to serve the needs of people locally, regionally and globally, be relational in your pursuits! God gave you your gifts to satisfy the welfare and needs of others. Your services, trades and abilities will help make the lives of those you are serving easier and happier.

1. Where did this river start?

We have come a long way from the days of bartering and gift economies when it comes to the valuation and exchange of services in society. In our money-driven world, the concept of simply doing something for someone at no charge, knowing that same someone will return the favor in the future, is nothing more than a historical, utopian dream. These early forms of exchange for services worked well in small communities. But as civilization expanded and population increased, more and more people were peddling their services to people they didn't know, who were often outside their communities. "Returning the favor" became problematic, if not impossible. As trade expanded from local and regional to international, a need arose for a service to loan and exchange money. The word *bank* came into use, which is in fact a Yiddish word meaning "bench" or "table." Today, commerce and consumer services are huge. The retail, distribution and shipping services of Amazon and Walmart make these industry giants among the largest consumer service businesses in the world.

2. Where is this river going?

Where is all this consumer service and commerce going? As the exchange of digital currencies continues to reshape the way we transact and conduct our business services, it will definitely get easier and faster. Cloud-based services for small business owners will continue to help them streamline their point of sales, payroll, personnel management, inventory control, bookkeeping and banking, allowing them to spend more time on their customers, clients and corporate accounts. As competition continues to drive this sector, those who deliver the best customer service experience will do well. You get one shot with consumers today, so make it count. From a biblical perspective, I would be remiss not to mention the eschatological revelation of the *ability to buy and sell* (see Revelation 13:17). As tech companies gain a greater stronghold on the way business is conducted globally, and as our culture becomes more and more spiritually and politically divided, there grows the potential for business discrimination. As an entrepreneur in the consumer services and commerce sector, find creative ways to be relational with your customers and clientele. Don't allow technology to drive your business.

Hell or High Water

1. How has the enemy polluted this river?

As Chris explained, this river of commerce and consumerism first flowed from the hearts of people in a gift economy who understood sowing and reaping. So what went wrong? I'll offer the perfect illustration, albeit creative: In the very first episode of *Little House on the Prairie*, "A Harvest of Friends," Charles Ingalls is new to Walnut Grove. While walking to work at the mill, he encounters a stranded Doc Baker and helps him by fixing his buggy wheel. When the doc introduces himself and offers to pay, Charles says, "No, thank you . . . just a ride into Walnut Grove would be fine." Doc obliges, but then later shows up at the mill with a cage full of chickens, which newcomer Charles obviously needs for a new farm, so he is grateful. It was the first *bona fide* transaction of their fiscal-family-friendship, which many communities operated on (this describes a relationship that is occasionally fiscal, feels like family and is a lifelong friendship). But what happens next is what began to pollute the commerce river. Charles has no cash for the plow or seed he needs, so he barters with a Mr. O'Neil, who needs a roof repair that Charles can provide in trade. Charles says, "I've got something you need more than money." When O'Neil asks what that could be, Charles answers, "Know-how. Enough to put a new roof on that shed." They shake hands on it, but only after O'Neil makes Charles sign an agreement to offer his oxen as collateral in case he doesn't complete the bargain. When Charles suffers a fall and breaks four ribs with only 99 percent of the work done, O'Neil takes advantage of Charles and claims the oxen (the modern-day equivalent of a car repossession), refusing him any more time. Were it not for all the townspeople who showed up to finish the other 1 percent of the work for their new friend, Charles, he would have lost everything, maybe even his life. He had sown friendship, so he had a harvest of friends who came through. But from this story you can see how easily the world began to abuse the beauty of a handshake agreement with greed and dishonest gain. And as transactions have become more sophisticated over time, so has the thievery. Is there anything God can do about it today? Absolutely! Read on . . .

2. How can God purify this river?

Chris was absolutely right when he advised, "Find creative ways to be relational with your customers and clientele. Don't allow technology to drive your business." That may seem impossible to do in our fast-paced, modern world, but if you are going to help purify this river—as either an entrepreneur or a laborer—then you will have to do two things: (1) Be a businessperson who will keep your word in this sector. And (2) Get *God's Word* back into it: "Better is a poor man who walks in his integrity than a rich man who is crooked in his ways" (Proverbs 28:6 ESV). Integrity alone is the cure for all greed, false advertising, forgery, price gouging, bribery, insider trading, antitrust violations, embezzlement, racketeering and other river pollutants such as bank, tax and insurance fraud.

Head above Water—Doctor's Orders

1. What are my health risks in this river?

This is a diverse sector, distinct from other sectors because it is less about a tangible product that you can hold in your hands, and more about a service you provide. So this industry's laborers will also have a diverse set of risks. But overall, there is one main common risk factor for people in this sector, because many in it sit down for a living—sometimes in a car or truck, but often at a desk for some part of the day. Specific stressors stem from that. In fact, an article in *Corporate Wellness Magazine* entitled "Workplace Stress: A Silent Killer of Employee Health and Productivity" says this:

> Workplace stressors are classified as physical and psychosocial. Physical stressors include noise, poor lighting, poor office or work layout, and ergonomic factors, such as bad working postures.

Psychosocial stressors are, arguably, the most predominant stress factors. These include high job demands, inflexible working hours, poor job control, poor work design and structure, bullying, harassments, and job insecurity. . . .

These effects occur in a continuum, beginning as distress in response to stressors. Distress, in turn, leads to elevated blood pressure and anxiety, which increase the risk of coronary heart disease, substance abuse, and anxiety disorders. . . .

There is also a growing body of evidence that work-related stress increases one's risk of diabetes. Other physical health problems linked to workplace stress include immune deficiency disorders, musculoskeletal disorders including chronic back pain, and gastrointestinal disorders, such as irritable bowel syndrome.

Workplace stress also has adverse effects on workers' mental health, with an increased risk of anxiety, burnout, depression, and substance use disorders. Workers who are stressed at work are more likely to engage in unhealthy behaviors, such as cigarette smoking, alcohol and drug abuse, and poor dietary patterns.[1]

2. How can I protect myself in this river—body, mind and spirit?

Physically and emotionally: The same article I just quoted went on to list a few practical solutions for such business stressors. The article calls these "primary interventions," and here are some examples:

- Redesigning the work environment
- Providing breaks and nap-times for employees
- Increasing employee participation in decision making and work planning
- Increasing time and resources for completing specific job tasks
- Creating clear promotion and reward pathways[2]

The article also suggests what are called "secondary interventions," such as these:

- Cognitive behavioral therapy training for workers

- Routine health surveillance—screening for high blood pressure and stress symptoms[3]

Should illness be present, "tertiary interventions" are recommended, such as these:

- Providing medical care and employee assistance programs to affected workers
- Return-to-work plans including modification and redesign of work[4]

Spiritually: Whatever career path you have chosen in this river—or if you are just sticking your toe in the water—remember that you don't need to strive or stress over your work. Listen to Proverbs 22:29 (NIV) and speak it over your life: "Do you see someone skilled in their work? They will serve before kings; they will not serve before officials of low rank."

The Coast Is Clear

How can my spiritual personality make an impact in this river?

The apostle personality: If you have the apostle personality, you are a trusted leader and capable manager in your industry, and in fact, with the right team members around you, you are capable of entrepreneurship. You have highly developed skills that can lead teams, departments and contractors underneath you, and you are able to do it efficiently, like a fast-flowing estuary. Delegation is your middle name, and people enjoy working for you. You are also ever mindful of keeping the client happy, and you have the high standard of making sure that those you lead make customer service a priority.

The prophet personality: If you have the prophet personality, you are valuable to co-leaders and team members for keeping morale up and for keeping the project or day moving in the right direction. You have a keen sense of when things are getting off course, and you are good at redirection. Yet be careful not to become critical in the process, and always find ways to encourage your co-workers first. You are keenly aware of customer satisfaction, and being the underground river that you are, you often find plenty of deep, meaningful ministry moments despite looming deadlines. You thrive on a little bit of stress, but pace yourself.

The evangelist personality: If you have the evangelist personality, you will be a phenomenal spokesperson. Because of the favor of God on your life, you will draw many to your company or business. This could translate to social media savvy that your co-workers do not have, creating a niche for you. You have the ability to communicate well, which will result in an internal trust with the people with whom you work. It could also translate into being successful in marketing or sales, should those interest you. You always know the right thing to say, and others admire your whitewater rapids enthusiasm.

The pastor personality: If you have the pastor personality, you will most likely find yourself in service industries that care directly for people. Even at the highest rung of the corporate ladder, your priority will always be the welfare of others. Whereas others around you see dollar signs, you see hearts and faces. But remember that it will take both you and these bottom-dollar others to fulfill your business goals and experience growth. You go the extra mile to see to it that your customers are taken care of, and you are also the gentle stream that runs to the office to care for your co-workers.

The teacher personality: If you have the teacher personality, you will spend a great deal of your time training others. Instruction is your middle name, and goal setting is your game. You love to-do lists and are full of information for helping to clearly communicate policies to your customers and expectations to your co-workers. You are the one who brings a project or problem into focus, and you are the troubleshooter everyone looks to for solutions. Your multitasking tributary mind will always need to remember to delegate so you don't burn yourself out by spreading yourself too thin.

Walk on Water (from God's Word)

He opened the rock and water flowed out;
It ran in the dry places like a river.

Psalm 105:41

Academics and Training River

Academics and training careers include (but are not limited to) these:

Academic positions:

Administrators

Assistant teachers

Bedels

Bursars

Bye-fellows

CEOs of public schools

Chancellors

Coaches

College professors

Correctional nursing

Curators

Deputy head teachers

Directors musices

Docents

Dominies
Educational technologists
Elementary school teachers
Employment counsellors
ESL (English as a second language) teachers
Exam invigilators
Executive head teachers
Fellows
Foreign language teachers
Global career development facilitators
Governesses
Graduate assistants
Head teachers
High masters
High school teachers
Housemasters
Information professionals
Kindergarten teachers

Lecturers
Medical education managers
Middle school teachers
Museum guide educators
Music directors
Paraprofessional educators
Parent educators (homeschool)
Porters (college)
Pracademics
Preschool teachers
Principals
Pro-chancellors
Professors
Professorial lecturers
Program directors
Provosts
Registrars
School counselors
School social workers
Superintendents

Non-academic vocational training:

Bible school or seminary
Carpentry
Catering management
Civil engineering tech
Construction management
Cosmetology
Culinary arts
Dental assisting
Diesel mechanics
Disaster management

Electricians
General automotive
HVAC repair
Machining
Massage therapy
Medical assisting
Medical coding
Plumbing
Theatre
Welding

Come to the River

You who have the mind and patience to teach, educate, train and mentor, you are an impact person! At every level of human development, you are ready with understanding and knowledge to inform, equip, inspire and prepare people to succeed in life. Your wisdom is respected, and your insights fill us with awe. You live to impart something of yourself to someone else. The impressions you make last a lifetime, and we owe much of our success to you, your patience and your desire to see us learn and grow.

1. Where did this river start?

Long before the first educational system or institution was built, families were the teachers in society. Learning in early civilization was provisional and centered around exploration and the development of skills like hunting, fishing and trapping. As agriculture developed, learning became labor-centered and required that people learn about how to plow the soil, how to plant, grow and harvest plants, and how to raise animals. People learned what they needed to learn to eat, have shelter and support a family. Education didn't stretch too far beyond the family's property line. Historically, a higher education was reserved for the wealthy, even as far back as 2400 BC in Egypt and 1600 BC in China. In Greece, Socrates developed the Socratic method of teaching in the fifth century BC. The Spartans were the first to develop military schools for boys, and they produced some of the most feared warriors in history. Plato and Aristotle developed academies for higher learning in the fourth century BC. Greece became a world leader in the propagation of modern education and academia around the world. During the Reformation, Martin Luther was instrumental in bringing biblical learning to the world. In the 1600s, education began to widen its banks to the masses in America with the founding of institutions like Harvard and William and Mary. Then there came the first printing of the children's schoolbook *The New England Primer*. And still, the education river was just getting started!

2. Where is this river going?

According to a report by Melanie Hanson with the Education Data Initiative, currently the average cost of college in the United States is $35,331 per student per year, including books, supplies and daily living expenses.[1] The cost is less for public state schools and higher for private four-year institutions. With the cost of higher education rising at a rate of almost 7 percent per year, will the value of attending a college campus reach a point of diminishing returns? It doesn't seem that way, with 46 million students and parents willing to put all their assets on the line to back the nearly $1.75 trillion dollars in student loan debt.[2] With the rise of online options for degree seekers, many will choose to find a more economical way to get a well-rounded education for jobs that don't require a marquee name on the degree. For more practical people wanting to enter the job marketplace quickly and without all that debt, training institutes, trade schools and associates degrees will become more attractive. These factors are things to consider as you make your way into the river of academics and training as an educator, trainer or mentor, and yes . . . even as a student!

Hell or High Water

1. How has the enemy polluted this river?

The topic of how worldwide education systems became corrupt is a matter of debate, but no country is exempt from the corruption. According to a report by Transparency International, the top five most corrupt school systems in the world are Russia, India, Japan, Indonesia and Mexico (this counts childhood education all the way up through secondary education).[3] Most analysts cite reductions in public funding as fueling the corruption. But many others cite just the opposite and are of the opinion that too much public funding is being spent at levels that are far removed from local private input. In another study, the annual Best Countries report conducted by *U.S. News & World Report*, thousands of people were surveyed across 78 countries. As of 2021, the ten countries voted to have the best education systems were these:

1. The United States
2. The United Kingdom
3. Germany
4. Canada
5. France
6. Switzerland
7. Japan
8. Australia
9. Sweden
10. The Netherlands[4]

Even though the United States tops the list as being best in education, however, American students consistently score lower in math and science than students from many other countries. In a 2018 *Business Insider* report, the Unites States ranked 38th in math scores and 24th in science.[5]

2. How can God purify this river?

Although the academics and training river includes much more than the education of our children, that is where it starts. Let's take a look at what God is doing there for just a minute. Oh, how far we have come from the days when a child's training was more personalized and tailor-made for them in private by their first teachers—their parents! In America, Massachusetts's Horace Mann birthed the common-school movement in the late 1800s, which pushed for public schools funded by local property taxes. It sounds noble enough a cause to educate children together, but a push was also made for a statewide curriculum and another levy to pay for it, which led to one person (with minimal input from a small school board) deciding what everyone would learn. Due to Mann's efforts, in the late 1800s public schools flourished, and children left their homes and congregated in classrooms. Once upon a time, 100 percent of children had been homeschooled. By the close of the 1800s, public schools outnumbered private learning environments. By the close of the 1900s (when I began homeschooling), that original 100 percent homeschool rate had dropped down to 1 percent. But think of it: During the pandemic of 2020, most schools closed globally. Suddenly, 100 percent of children were homeschooled again. Parents all over the world were homeschooling under duress, but many were surprised to learn that they preferred it since it freed them from the 100-year practice of having just a few individuals form the thoughts and opinions of their children. Homeschooling has now tripled in the last three years and has taken a meteoric leap back up to 11 percent.[6] I would like to think that God could purify this river by bringing about a worldwide return to in-home education in the majority of homes. And how ideal it would be for those who still choose public education, if godly educators (like maybe yourself) jumped into this academics river and cleansed the wicked waters that our children are drowning in. At the time of this writing, some children are being taught with school curriculum asserting that when babies are born, doctors take a "guess" at gender and sometimes get it wrong. Therefore, the babies may not have been assigned the right gender. And such diabolical agendas have reached all the way to our college campuses, where conservative Christian voices are censored. *Now* is the time for brave voices of righteousness to arise! How else will we put an end to extreme and ungodly "woke" ideologies being taught to the masses, shaping future generations to perpetuate these beliefs?

Head above Water—Doctor's Orders

1. What are my health risks in this river?

Did you notice from the career paths and industry options at the front pages of this chapter that no two teachers are alike? Some are museum tour guides and some are college deans. Some are cosmetology instructors and others are high school principals. Whether in an academic institution or a vocational training center, teachers are the primary gatekeepers for many eager young minds. Depending on where they teach, there will be different health risks. An article published by Pennsylvania State University, "Teacher Stress and Health," draws some common ground for all teachers. It says,

Teaching is one of the most stressful occupations in the country, but introducing organizational and individual interventions can help minimize the negative effects of teacher stress. . . .
- Forty-six percent of teachers report high daily stress, which compromises their health, sleep, quality of life, and teaching performance.
- When teachers are highly stressed, students show lower levels of both social adjustment and academic performance.
- Interventions on the organizational or individual level, or those that reach both, can help reduce teacher stress by changing the culture and approach to teaching.[7]

The bottom line is that stressed-out teachers affect educational outcomes and wind up harming society in the end, not to mention harming the organizations that employ them.

2. How can I protect myself in this river—body, mind and spirit?

Physically: If you are planning a career as an educator, do your homework (no pun intended) on the space you will be teaching in and make sure it is a safe place for you to spend the majority of your day. This is true whether you are a welding instructor or a private governess.

Emotionally: Find ways to combat stress!

Spiritually: Allow God to use you as an educator for His glory. An article entitled "Will You Lose Your Faith in College?" cites a Barna study that is particularly alarming:

Barna estimates that roughly 70% of high school students who enter college as professing Christians will leave with little to no faith. These students usually don't return to their faith even after graduation, as Barna projects that 80% of those reared in the church will be "disengaged" by the time they are 29.[8]

Students are leaving college in both debt and doubt. If you have plans to enter this occupational river, whether you spend four hours with individuals or four years, make the intentional commitment to guard the faith of those students in your care (young and old). Commit to doing everything within your power to let them leave your tutelage stronger in their faith than when they came to you.

The Coast Is Clear

How can my spiritual personality make an impact in this river?

The apostle personality: If you have the apostle personality, you are a teacher of teachers. Although you are capable of teaching, one of your primary functions will be the placement of other teachers, bringing them on board or raising them up. You will gravitate toward seats of authority and be responsible for other educators. Being the estuary that you are, you will facilitate them in all coming together with your help, despite their different ideologies and areas of expertise. Depending on the level of confidence you are willing to embrace from God, you have the self-governing tendencies that make you a natural-born education entrepreneur.

The prophet personality: If you have the prophet personality, you are a deep thinker amongst your peers and are the underground river that provides the necessary creative vision that those around you need. You are the forward-thinking philosopher, theologian and realist—maybe even a bit mysterious or enigmatic. Even if you are in trade industry training, your depth of knowledge makes you a bit of a celebrity in your field. You are an inspiration to your students, but might be considered a dreamer by your contemporaries because you are the quintessential creative educator who thinks outside the box.

The evangelist personality: If you have the evangelist personality, expect to be center stage often in your field of education. In fact, you will rise to the top of this river fast. If teachers are to inspire their students, then you are the inspirer of the inspirers, and you bring the kind of encouraging training that educators underneath you need. Whether you are in the boardroom, classroom or conference room, your whitewater rapid charisma holds the attention of everyone you teach. Any problems that arise at work are less likely to be with your adoring students than with jealous peers.

The pastor personality: If you have the pastor personality, you are a natural-born counselor and advisor. You understand that people don't care what you know until they know that you care, and you genuinely care about more than just the education of those entrusted to you. Whereas other educators see students' minds and intellects, you see their hearts and souls. You enjoy one-on-one interactions, even if you have to be in front of groups often. You are the gentle stream running through the hallways, and both your co-workers and students respect how you flow so effortlessly between their teacher and friend.

The teacher personality: If you have the teacher personality, you are like a fish in water, so to speak, in this river! You make learning fun and love what you do, and the world is your classroom because you can turn anything—absolutely anything—into a teachable moment. As a tributary, you are a walking encyclopedia on whatever your current passion is. You have the ability to turn the mundane into something miraculous. If you are an actual educator, then yours is the class everyone wants to sign up for. If you are not in the classroom, because you have made your way to the top, a part of you will always miss your students.

Walk on Water (from God's Word)

The Spirit and the bride say, "Come." And let the one who hears say, "Come." And let the one who is thirsty come; let the one who wishes take the water of life without cost.

Revelation 22:17

Press and
Telecommunications River

Press and telecommunications industry careers include (but are not limited to) these:

Press and telecommunications:

Cable networks

Cable providers

Cell phone providers

Data processing and hosting services

Database and directory publications

Database, storage and backup publications

Digital media

E-book publishing

Email (digital) providers

Ethics and interactive media

Integrated communication

Interactive media

Internet publishing and broadcasting

Internet radio broadcasting

Internet service providers
Journalism
News syndicates
Newspaper publishing
Political journalism
Radio
Radio broadcasting
Satellite telecommunications
   providers
Satellite TV providers
Search engines
Security software publishing

Social media
Software publishing
Telecommunications
   resellers
Telephone service providers
Television
Television broadcasting
Wired telecommunications
   carriers
Wireless telecommunications
   carriers

Connected Careers:

Assignment editors
Columnists
Community correspondents
Conservation photographers
Copy editing
Copywriting
Correspondents
Courtroom sketching
Editing
Editorial boards
Fact-checking
Food critics
Gossip columnists
Illustrators
Journalists
Mailers
Military journalism (in the
   United States)

Mojos (mobile journalist)
Muckrakers
News analysts
News anchors
News contributors
News directors
News presenters
Newspaper typesetters
Podcasters
Photojournalists
Political editors
Press secretaries
Proofreaders
Speechwriters
Staff writers
Style guides
Wire editors

Come to the River

You who have a heart and mind to alert the masses, proclaim truth and shed light into culture for the benefit of others, God has gifted you with a voice that commands our attention, and a perspective that enlightens our minds and brings truth to our spirits! You were created to speak the truth in love, with courage and integrity.

1. Where did this river start?

From the beginning of time, humankind's curiosity and the desire to "know" has fueled a wide variety of forms of news gathering, communication and broadcasting. One of the most fascinating forms of communication, used as early as 3000 BC by the Egyptians, is homing pigeons or carrier pigeons. Carrying a small message tied to their leg, these amazing birds have been known to be able to return to their nests from as far away as 1,100 miles at a speed of 60 to 120 miles per hour. News traveled fast even then! To spread news in a kingdom where illiteracy was the norm, "town criers" were sent as official representatives of the king. The phrase "don't shoot the messenger" was a legitimate warning because any harm done to a town crier was considered an act of treason against the king. The Chinese are credited with building the earliest printing press, but it is Johann Gutenberg from Germany who invented the moveable-type printing press that ushered in the Reformation through the first printing of the Bible in 1455. Communication and the press have always been vital for the preservation and advancement of civilization. Shared information empowers people to perceive, to learn and to make conclusive, life-changing decisions. Without free speech and freedom of the press, civil liberties would disappear. From the homing pigeons to the Reformation to smartphones to whatever new gadgets are yet to be imagined, cultures will always depend on knowledge and the Good News for survival.

2. Where is this river going?

Forty years ago, author John Naisbitt said in his *New York Times* bestselling book *Megatrends: Ten New Directions*

Transforming Our Lives, "We are drowning in information but starved for knowledge."[1] His words could not be any truer today. It is the blessing and the curse. Much more recently, an article entitled "Too Much Information, Too Little Time" tells us,

> Scientists have measured the amount of data that enter the brain and found that an average person living today processes as much as 74 GB in information a day (that is as much as watching 16 movies), through TV, computers, cell phones, tablets, billboards, and many other gadgets. Every year it is about 5% more than the previous year. Only 500 years ago, 74 GB of information would be what a highly educated person consumed in a lifetime, through books and stories.[2]

It doesn't appear that there will be a shortage of supply or demand anytime soon, but the question remains: Where is all this information leading us as a society? As this press and telecommunications river continues to flood its banks, content developers in this sector will need to consider ways to dam up the flow of information and begin thinking of ways to positively impact society with knowledgeable, less divisive commentary, and with programming that edifies and unifies. Though it will always be the goal of the press to "find a great story," the outlets that make it their goal to "find a great *true* story" will rise in favor, ratings and market share.

Hell or High Water

1. How has the enemy polluted this river?

Although this river is often referred to as "the media," we steered clear of that in this chapter's title because the phrase is also sometimes perceived as pertaining to those in entertainment or on television in general. Not everybody who appears on your TV is in the media! We are reserving its meaning here for members of the press, whatever their individual medium: television, radio, newspaper, the Internet, etc. And we have put the "telecommunications" industry in this same river since none of those who work in the press could do their jobs without those who work in telecommunications media. This river dovetails very closely with the information technology (IT) river as well. But whereas everyone in the press uses technology, not everyone in technology is in the press. So that is our distinction here. It also helps us narrow down the pollutants in this river to a distinct few. We earlier identified the floating filth of the IT river to be things like online gambling, scamming, illegal downloading, online predators, malware, identity theft, hacking, the loss of privacy, Internet addiction and more. Yet this press and telecommunications river is less polluted by individuals and more by conglomerates. You have entire cable networks devoted to the dissemination of embellished and biased news. The trending phrase for this is "fake news," or the "fake media." I have wondered many times if this will play out to be the "false prophet" that Revelation speaks of (see Revelation 19:20; 20:10). In a moment, we will look at that and talk about how you can protect yourself from him or it, if you are going to work in this river, or even if you just live on Planet Earth! It is easy to see how this river flows through every home in the world and from every smartphone and TV.

2. How can God purify this river?

With truth. And if you are going to work in this river, you must be a conduit of truth. As partisan press members, global tech companies and their lobbyists partner with misguided governmental bureaucrats who have less than pure motives, they are partnering to shut down, censor and cancel those who oppose them. And even worse than being censored is for our Good News of the Kingdom to be labeled as hate speech. But every now and again, you see a brave soul and member of the press stand up for truth. For example, a few years ago as a new president took office, his new press secretary took the podium for the first time at a White House briefing and was asked this question by a reporter: "Will you ever lie to us?" Her answer was that she absolutely would never lie to them. I was watching from home and wished that on top of that answer she would have added, "And do you, as a member of the press, promise never to lie to the American people? In fact, may I have a show of hands of every reporter who vows never to lie to the American people?" I was hoping she could hear me prompting her through the television screen, but that's not how it played out. Besides, there probably would not have been many hands raised. So how can God purify this river? Through His people in it who are committed to the truth. You can raise your hand right now and take a vow never to lie to the public. Wherever you are right now, raise your hand and commit that so far as it depends on you, you will not partake in fear-mongering, control, manipulation or lies. Choose integrity, accuracy, truth and free speech.

Head above Water—Doctor's Orders

1. What are my health risks in this river?

If you are going to be in this press and telecommunications river, you are going to play an important role in the last days, before the return of Christ. As a result, your greatest health risks will be to your spiritual health as you swim upstream toward the Spirit of truth through many cesspools of deceit. As I mentioned previously, I am of the belief that the fake news is akin to the false prophet from the book of Revelation. I will explain why after we read Revelation 13:11–18:

> Then I saw another beast coming up out of the earth; and he had two horns like a lamb and he spoke as a dragon. He exercises all the authority of the first beast in his presence. And he makes the earth and those who dwell in it to worship the first beast, whose fatal wound was healed. He performs great signs, so that he even makes fire come down out of heaven to the earth in the presence of men. And he deceives those who dwell on the earth because of the signs which it was given him to perform in the presence of the beast, telling those who dwell on the earth to make an image to the beast who had the wound of the sword and has come to life. And it was given to him to give breath to the image of the beast, so that the image of the beast would even speak and cause as many as do not worship the image of the beast to be killed. And he causes all, the small and the great, and the rich and the poor, and the free men and the slaves, to be given a mark on their right hand or on their forehead, and he provides that no one will be able to buy or to sell,

except the one who has the mark, either the name of the beast or the number of his name. Here is wisdom. Let him who has understanding calculate the number of the beast, for the number is that of a man; and his number is six hundred and sixty-six.

I explained in chapter 12 how the number 666 has a Hebraic equivalent of "www." You can take a moment to reread that section since it pertains to the Internet's role in the end times, but also know this about the above passage and the press/media in the last days: Just as there is a Holy Trinity, Revelation 13 shows us that in the end days there will be an unholy trinity comprised of Satan, the Antichrist and the false prophet. This is in direct rebellion to the Holy Trinity comprised of God, Jesus and the Holy Spirit. If we begin to view the false prophet through the lens of his activities, we see that many of them are the definition of what the press does. In fact, earlier in Revelation 13 we find a description about the Antichrist that reads, "His fatal wound was healed. And the whole earth was amazed and followed after the beast" (verse 3). So ask yourself, how else can the whole earth know about something unless the press and media are involved? We see here that the media will surely propagate the lies and false miracles of the Antichrist, leading the masses astray. Now, listen again to some of these phrases from that Revelation 13 passage about the false prophet (italics mine), keeping all that in mind about "him" being the press or members of the media:

He *spoke* as a dragon. . . . He makes *the earth* and those who dwell in it to worship the first beast, whose fatal wound was healed. He performs *great signs*. . . . He *deceives those who dwell on the earth* because of the signs . . . *telling those who dwell on the earth* to make an image to the beast. . . . And it was given to him to *give breath to the image of the beast, so that the image of the beast would even speak* and cause as many as do not worship the image of the beast to be killed.

And with all those things in mind, let me speak next to your personal protection in this river.

2. How can I protect myself in this river—body, mind and spirit?

Physically, emotionally and spiritually: There is only one antidote for deceit, and that is *truth*. The Holy Spirit is known in the Bible as the Spirit of truth. If you are going to work in this industry, you are going to have to stay very full of the Holy Spirit and have a strong commitment to honesty—in private and in public. Remain in close accountability to a local church and receive prayer often from the pastor and a team who cover you, since you will definitely be on the front lines in the last days. This cannot be stressed enough: *Choose truth.* No matter what it costs you, choose truth.

The Coast Is Clear

How can my spiritual personality make an impact in this river?

The apostle personality: If you have the apostle personality, you will find yourself in a place of cultural influence beyond your wildest imagination. Many "streams" of thought and opinion will filter through your estuary, giving new meaning in your life to the words *mainstream* and *livestream.* You will likely have decision-making responsibilities over both. Many judgment calls will come down to your final word on the matter, and you will often be the final gatekeeper of truth. Make the commitment never to commission false prophets or disciples of deceit. Choose truth at every juncture—despite your political persuasion—and have a zero-tolerance policy for anything less.

The prophet personality: If you have the prophet personality, then you likely have communication and writing skills that you could have put to use in the creativity river, but you have chosen this press and telecommunications river that influences the governance of the world powers large and small. Your underwater river research exposes deep corruption and replaces it with the truth, but your steps in doing so will have to be calculated with caution. Each keystroke and stroke of your pen is like a stroke swimming upstream in this critical river. The false prophet's words will be all around you, but your words will drown those out with truth.

The evangelist personality: If you have the evangelist personality, many eyes and ears are on you. What will you say? How will you answer? Yours is a life of rehearsed spontaneity in this industry, and you will be able to speak unpopular truths because of your whitewater rapids charisma and communication skills. Use this to your advantage and for God's gain alone. You will need thick skin in these frigid waters. You may have distinct seasons of platform visibility, but don't succumb to the celebrity undertow. Stay on course with your two oars of humility and truth.

The pastor personality: If you have the pastor personality, you are the heart in an industry full of mouths. You are a lifeline to the drowning and a lifeboat to the perishing in this river. Some are dying of reputational homicide, others by scandal, and others by their own transgressions, but your words and actions will bring revelation to everyone around you about how temporal this life is and how our eyes must stay fixed above, on the eternal. In an industry drenched with bad news, you are the deliverer of Good News, and you are this industry's constant gentle stream of hope.

The teacher personality: If you have the teacher personality, you have the gift of making a media message out of every mess you see. You can bring clarity to the most difficult of topics, and bring an informative perspective to every crisis. Your expertise is sought after to extract truth from confusion. Pray that your level of character matches your level of wisdom so that you might never fall from the graces of the public that God has given you and lose their respect and audience. Remember that each avenue of your tributary career is full of students swimming in the wake of your influential current.

Walk on Water (from God's Word)

> There is a river whose streams make glad the city of God,
> The holy dwelling places of the Most High.
>
> Psalm 46:4

Energy and Utilities River

Energy and utility industry careers include (but are not limited to) these:

Battery recycling
Bioenergy production
Biomass production
Carbon capture and storage
Civil engineering
Coal and natural gas power
Coal mining
Copper, nickel, lead and
  zinc mining
Consumable fuels
Crude oil drilling
Diesel fuel

Electric companies
Electric power
  transmission
Electric vehicle charging
  stations
Electrical engineering
Enabling technologies
Energy equipment industry
Energy fuel drilling
Energy research and
  development
Energy network operators

Energy service providers and retailers

Energy traders and marketers

Environmental engineering

Ethanol fuel production

Fossil fuel production

Gasoline

Geothermal electricity plant operation

Geothermal production

Gold and silver ore mining

Heating oils

Hydroelectric power

Hydrogen production

Hydropower production

Industrial engineering

Iron or mining

Laboratory and testing services

Lithium battery manufacturing

Mechanical engineering

Mineral and phosphate mining

Mining

Molybdenum and metal ore mining

Natural gas companies

Natural gas distribution

Nuclear engineering

Nuclear power

Oil and gas field services

Oil drilling and gas extraction

Petroleum products and oil

Photovoltaics production

Pipeline refining

Power generation

Renewable energy

Sand and gravel mining

Sanitation/waste disposal companies

Sewage removal companies

Sewage treatment facilities

Solar energy production

Solar farm development

Solar panel production

Solar power

Solar radiation production

Sonar device manufacturing

Steam and air conditioning supply

Stone mining

Thermal and chemical energy

Tire and rubber recycling

Toxic waste management

Waste-to-energy production

Water supply and irrigation systems

Water supply companies

Wind power

Wind turbine development

Come to the River

You, with the inquisitive mind and the brains to understand the complexities of science and math, and who loves to explore the furthest reaches of innovation—you are the energy and utility pioneer of the future. You are an explorer, an innovator, a problem solver. The world is looking to you to make our world safer and cleaner, and to make it run more efficiently.

1. Where did this river start?

From a biblical view, energy began with God. In His master plan for humanity, God knew that every living thing would require energy to live and be sustained. The first two verses of the book of Genesis describe the earth as formless, void and dark, and say that the Spirit of God was *hovering* or *moving* over the face of the deep. Physicists agree that wind, though unseen, has mass, and that when something that has mass moves, it has kinetic energy. Kinetic energy is the energy of motion. It is logical, then, to assume that the movement of the Spirit over the waters, like wind, was creating energy for the very first time on the face of the earth. Then God said, "Let there be light" (Genesis 1:3), and the world was introduced to another form of energy—the sun. The sun is the most powerful source of energy in our solar system. It produces light and heat through the perpetual fusion of hydrogen atoms into helium atoms. As the tiny atoms collide within the sun, they create a tremendous amount of energy—the very power of the sun, in fact. As one scientist put it, "Every second the sun produces the same energy as about a trillion megaton bombs! In one second, our sun produces enough energy for almost 500,000 years of the current needs of our so-called civilization. If only we could collect it all and use it!"[1] Throughout history, humankind has been harnessing the power of water, wind, the sun and fossil fuels to advance civilization. Yet there is still so much for us to learn about the various life-sustaining elements of energy that have been with us from the very beginning.

215

2. Where is this river going?

As we continue to debate the questions surrounding our future use of renewable and nonrenewable energy resources, some untapped avenues are getting very little attention. I want to highlight some of them here. If you have not heard of the hydrogen-powered cars yet, you will. Fuel cell electric vehicles (FCEVs) run on stored hydrogen that is converted to electricity and emits only water vapor and warm air. Much like electric vehicles, they have a current range of about 300 miles. Another alternative is electromagnetic propulsion. If you have ever tried to put two strong magnets together, you can feel the push or pull of the invisible magnetic force in the magnets as their polarities try to attract or resist. This energy is being used to power vehicles and trains. The Japanese Maglev, or magnetic levitating train, uses an electrodynamic suspension system that allows the train to actually levitate, reducing friction. It can reach a top speed of 375 mph. Geothermal and magma power utilize the energy in the earth's core for heating and cooling, and even for generating electricity. Embeddable solar is gaining traction due to its ability to be embedded in window glass in such a way so as not to block visibility, while still harvesting solar energy. There are so many ways for us to generate and store energy. Our greatest challenge will be finding successful ways to roll them out and make them consumer friendly.

Hell or High Water

1. How has the enemy polluted this river?

First, take a look at the various types of energy and the creative sources of power that our creative-genius God has miraculously placed in the earth and in its atmosphere for us. Energy.gov supplied the following information on "Capacity Factor by Energy Source in 2020":

- Nuclear—92.5 percent
- Geothermal—74.3 percent
- Natural gas—56.6 percent

- Hydropower—41.5 percent
- Coal—40.2 percent
- Wind—35.4 percent
- Solar—24.9 percent[2]

Regarding this data, the Office of Nuclear Energy explains,

> As you can see, nuclear energy has by far the highest capacity factor of any other energy source. This basically means nuclear power plants are producing maximum power more than 92 percent of the time during the year.
>
> That's about nearly 2 times more as natural gas and coal units, and almost 3 times or more reliable than wind and solar plants.
>
> Nuclear power plants are typically used more often because they require less maintenance and are designed to operate for longer stretches before refueling (typically every 1.5 or 2 years).[3]

So then, if nuclear energy is truly the bomb (pun intended), then why does that come with such a hazardous reputation, and how has this river's number one power source become so dangerous? The Kiwi Energy company offers several cons to nuclear energy, including radioactive waste, the negative impact on the environment, and what they call "risk of accident." Their website makes the important point that "Chernobyl, Three Mile Island, and Fukushima Daiichi are disasters that nobody wants to experience ever again under any circumstances."[4] The 1986 Chernobyl meltdown—history's worst nuclear disaster—took the lives of more than 50 people, including workers and first responders, with dozens more later contracting radiation sicknesses and dying. Somewhere between 50 and 185 million curies of radionuclides were released into the atmosphere—several times more radioactive than the atomic bombs dropped on Nagasaki and Hiroshima in Japan. This fallout spread via the wind all the way to Belarus, Russia and Ukraine, and as far west as France and Italy. But what many people don't know is that this tragic nuclear disaster was caused by human error—namely, sleep deprivation. That's right, worker fatigue.[5]

2. How can God purify this river?

To be honest, the greatest purification that needs to come to this energy river is not just in the "risk of accident" occurrences within its multiple power industries, but to the political debate itself over which power source is superior. All of God's power sources are miraculous, and none need to be excluded as part of His solution for our current-day energy crises—especially when it means that a nation can become energy independent and not have to fill the coffers of foreign nations that have less-than-peaceful agendas. Every political administration in every country wants to be the administration to say that its country did become energy independent, but none can get the masses to agree on which energy source is the best overall in terms of performance and the creation of jobs, along with renewable or nonrenewable energy. Health risks are also a consideration, which we will discuss next.

Head above Water—Doctor's Orders

1. What are my health risks in this river?

The online article "Health and safety in the energy sector," by Bectu (a United Kingdom trade union), says this:

> Generating, transmitting and distributing sources of power comes with inherent danger. In recent years the industry has made improvements in reducing the number of injuries, and the active involvement of reps has been key to this.
>
> While good progress has been made on safety, progress has not been so positive in addressing work-related health problems. Figures from the Health and Safety Executive show that the sector has one of the highest rates of occupational ill health across the whole economy.
>
> The networks industry's own figures show the number of days lost to sickness absence per worker has generally risen in recent years and now stands around 75% higher than the average across all sectors. A large amount of this absence is caused by musculo-skeletal disorders and mental health problems.[6]

And since we just mentioned fatigue and the Chernobyl disaster, I will add that Bectu named fatigue as a main culprit of risk in this entire industry, stating,

> Energy is a high hazard industry, so it is vital that anything which impedes an individual's ability to make sound operational decisions is thoroughly assessed and carefully managed.
>
> Fatigue is one such factor—it can result in slower reactions, reduced ability to process information and underestimation of risk, leading to errors and accidents, ill-health and injury. . . .
>
> . . . Research has shown that energy sector employees are struggling with fatigue, potentially putting themselves and their colleagues at risk.
>
> One in five respondents to our recent survey said that at some point in the past year they had felt too fatigued to work safely. Of these, three in five did not feel comfortable telling their employer.[7]

2. How can I protect myself in this river—body, mind and spirit?

Physically: Mobile Medical Corporation says this about the energy and utilities sector:

> Power and utilities keep our communities running efficiently each and every day, without us having to give it a second thought. The power and utility industry has a number of different sectors that fall under this umbrella such as water, electricity, and waste management, to name a few. Different work settings have their own set of occupational safety concerns and each environment should aim to tailor their resources to benefit the wellbeing of their employees.
>
> Fall hazards, exposure to dangerous materials or toxic substances, misuse of machinery, and many other risks in this industry call for specialized occupational health and safety services.[8]

Mobile Medical goes on to suggest the following services for optimum on-site safety: (1) rapid mobilization, (2) round-the-clock care, (3) hearing conservation, (4) respiratory protection, and (5) substance abuse testing.[9]

Emotionally: Be on guard against fatigue and the use and abuse of substances and stimulants as a solution to stay awake. Seek help for stimulant addictions.

Spiritually: Whether you choose a career path in renewable or non-renewable energy, remember that God made it all. Show respect for His diverse design for energy, and see all its forms as gifts from Him.

The Coast Is Clear

How can my spiritual personality make an impact in this river?

The apostle personality: If you have the apostle personality, you will commission teams underneath you, and you may even have one foot in this river and the other in another river such as politics and law, or the military/paramilitary—a convergence. You definitely have the administrative and communication skills for this, although you may be needed at a more local level. An estuary in your industry, you will often find its three key elements—generation, networks and retail—flowing across your desk into one stream. You have a reputation for getting the job done with excellence.

The prophet personality: If you have the prophet personality, you are a voice for change. You have a vision for the future of energy (or even for your own department) and can see far down this river's path. You will have to become fluent in the languages of all the other personalities in order to execute this vision and troubleshoot difficulties that arise. You are an underground river with a wealth of information about your industry. As it pertains to your particular area of expertise, your hard-earned wisdom earns you the authority to speak into each project with clarity.

The evangelist personality: If you have the evangelist personality, you are often put in the position of communicating the cutting-edge ideas that keep this river flowing. Your gift of persuasion affords you a high success rate in convincing others about new directions and techniques, unless you are also met with another evangelist personality who has an opposing opinion and has been commissioned to come and convince *you*. Stand your ground with your God-given convictions, and your greatest critics will become your new ideology converts, and perhaps your spiritual disciples. Your whitewater rapids magnetism makes you a natural fit for anything from sales to a Senate sub-committee.

The pastor personality: If you have the pastor personality, you are a gentle giant in an industry made of steel. Your main objective is delivering the power of God to individuals one by one to transform their lives. Whether you read meters, contracts or research data, you have the ability to take on the impossible because of your faith in Christ, and your genuine love of people usually puts you in the right place at the right time with the right solution. Remember that you are the gentle stream in this energetic river that is always rushing toward the future.

The teacher personality: If you have the teacher personality, you are both teacher and student in this ever-changing, innovative industry. Whether you are in the generation, extraction, conversion, storage, distribution or recycling of energy, instruction flows freely through your tributary teachings and enlightens many. Stand your ground with your critics and comfort the climate-change enthusiasts with the truth that we are one day getting a new heaven and a new earth: "Then I saw 'a new heaven and a new earth,' for the first heaven and the first earth had passed away. . . . He who was seated on the throne said, 'I am making everything new!'" (Revelation 21:1, 5 NIV).

Walk on Water (from God's Word)

Then he showed me a river of the water of life, clear as crystal, coming from the throne of God and of the Lamb, in the middle of its street. On either side of the river was the tree of life, bearing twelve kinds of fruit, yielding its fruit every month; and the leaves of the tree were for the healing of the nations.

Revelation 22:1–2

Ministries
and Charities River

Ministries and charities careers include (but are not limited to) serving in these organizations:

Association of Gospel
   Rescue Missions

Bible societies

Billy Graham Evangelistic
   Association

Campus Crusade for Christ

Celebrate Recovery

Charity nonprofits

Charity/special project
   fund-raising

Christian colleges

Christian drug rehab centers

Christian labor
   organizations

Christian media
   organizations

Christian mission hospitals

Christian orders and societies

Christian political organizations

Christian relief organizations

Christian resource materials

Christian schools (primary)

Christian schools (secondary)

Christian sports organizations

Christian Trade Union Federation of Germany

Christian trade unions

Christian Workers' Union

Christian youth organizations

Church planting

Churches

Congregations by country

Cross International

French Confederation of Christian Workers

Humanitarian aid

Jewish nonprofits

Mission organizations

Missionaries

Monasteries, abbeys, priories and friaries

Orphanages and group homes

Religious alliances and advocates

Religious broadcasting

Religious media production companies

Religious nonprofits

Religious public relations

Religious publishing organizations

Samaritan's Purse

Solidarity (South African trade union)

Spanish missions

Team Expansion

Television ministries

The Salvation Army

WEC International

World Confederation of Labour

World Movement of Christian Workers

World Relief

World Vision

World Vision United States

Worldwide Paraministries

Young Christian Workers

Youth with a Mission (YWAM)

Career Positions:
(Again, not an exhaustive list.)

Apostles	Music ministers
Assistant pastors	Pastors
Associate pastors	Teachers
Chaplains	Teacher/professors
Counselors	Worship directors
Deacons	
Elders	Worship leaders
Evangelists	Worship pastors
Missionaries	Writers

Come to the River

You who have a heart for ministry and charitable causes, and who may have one foot in industry and another foot in a different spot such as the river of creativity, or the river of education, or the river of telecommunications or the river of healthcare—you desire to devote your life to be God's earthly hands and feet to humanity through compassionate acts, missions, teaching and serving. We have intentionally placed this chapter last in the book. It is last not because the ministries/charities river is less important, but because we wanted you to wade through all the other eleven rivers first to help you see if you are truly supposed to be in this ministry river, or if you are to take ministry into the marketplace.

1. Where did this river start?

As I thought about where this river started, my mind went back to Israel's beginning as a nation. As God led 603,550 adult men, and an untold number of women and children, out of Egypt toward their Promised Land, Moses was tasked with the huge responsibility of establishing laws and ordinances for this massive wave of people. These laws and ordinances created a framework through which the nation could maintain order, promote civility and worship God.

Holiness before God was central to this "chosen" people, and the commandments and ordinances were specifically designed as a means through which each person could maintain right standing with God through offerings and sacrifices. The Tabernacle (housing the Ark of the Covenant and the Ten Commandments) was symbolically placed in the center of the camp, with all the tribes encamped around it. The tribe of Levi was the only tribe that had not worshiped the golden calf, and was therefore selected to be the remnant of Israel to represent the priesthood of God to the people. The Levites were in charge of the Temple and worship. All the tribes were allotted an inheritance of land in Canaan, but the Levites were not. They were responsible for some cities, but they could not be landowners, because the Lord was to be their inheritance: "For the LORD your God has chosen him [the Levite] and his sons from all your tribes, to stand and serve in the name of the LORD forever" (Deuteronomy 18:5). This is where the ministry river began.

2. Where is this river going?

From the days of the Levites to today, Judaism and Christianity have maintained this format in some fashion. Receiving the call to be "set apart" to minister and serve the Lord as a life pursuit is still reflected in our culture today. It is a vocation that comes with sacrifices, so careful consideration must be given before jumping into this river! In many ways like the Levites, people who sacrificially enter the waters of ministry and charity depend on the faithfulness and generosity of the rest of their nation for support. With a growing number of people losing faith in church leadership, this river needs apostles, prophets, evangelists, pastors and teachers who are full of faith and integrity. The nations are looking for guidance and want to trust the Church and its message. This river is turbulent, but it is destined to endure to the end by the grace of God, until every nation has heard, seen, felt and tasted the goodness of the Father, the Son and the Holy Spirit. As long as there are people who can endure hardship, remain full of integrity, walk in accountability and have enduring faith until the return of Jesus, there will be a river of ministries and charities in the earth.

Hell or High Water

1. How has the enemy polluted this river?

Satan despises this river. It is full of those who harm his mission, and he will try to drown them or drag their reputations over the rocks at every opportunity. This river is teeming with apostles, prophets, evangelists, pastors and teachers, not to mention Christian businessmen and businesswomen, educators, broadcasters, orphanage directors and countless overseers of charitable nonprofits. You'd think it would be the industry river with the cleanest water, but the truth is that it can be just as polluted as any secular river. Or maybe the pollution is just more visible to those watching from the banks and scrutinizing every move of the people within it. But it is obvious that the enemy has contaminated our waters with sin, or more specifically, the acceptance of it. Unfortunately, ministers try to justify their transgressions by convincing themselves that their work is vital and that surely God understands their need for occasional indulgences. At the time of this writing, it looks as though the 2020s will go down in history as one of the worst decades for ministry leaders to date. Pastors falling into sexual sin. Evangelists being investigated for financial fraud. Worship leaders "deconstructing" and diving headlong into total apostasy. Whole church denominations splitting over the ordination of homosexual leaders. Decades ago, I had a pastor I admired fall into such reprobate sin that it grieved thousands, and many hundreds fell with him. The Church in general has an issue with Christian celebrity—which borders on idolatry—and oh, how the mighty have fallen. Surveys from the Fuller Institute, George Barna, Lifeway, the Schaeffer Institute of Leadership Development, and *Christianity Today* were all recently combined for an insightful article called "Statistics in the Ministry" that can be found on the Pastoral Care Inc. website.[1] The statistics I talk about in the rest of this chapter all come from that article. But I begin with the statistic of how 66 percent of people expect a minister and his or her family to live with a higher moral standard than they do. That means people are watching us. That means they need us to lead the way. When we don't lead, they feel justified in leaving their faith behind entirely. The study reveals this truth and our trending bad fruit:

- 4,000 new churches begin each year and 7,000 churches close.
- Over 1,500 pastors left the ministry every month last year.
- Over 1,300 pastors were terminated by the local church each month, many without cause.
- Over 3,500 people a day left the church last year.

2. How can God purify this river?

Although many have fallen, many have stood! A revival of holiness is happening because the Holy Spirit is no longer the most neglected member of the Trinity in many churches. And remember, His main job is to make you holy! As we become full of this Spirit of holiness, Galatians 5 says we also become full of the fruits of the Spirit such as self-control, love and joy. It is obvious that we must turn the tide, and it is even one of our main motivations for writing this book. Our prayer is that you will jump into your river—whatever river that is (or rivers)—swim upstream and grow the Kingdom of God, not shrink it.

Head above Water—Doctor's Orders

1. What are my health risks in this river?

This river is ripe with health risks—body, mind and spirit. Just look at these statistics, and then we will discuss solutions:

- 38% of pastors are thinking of quitting the ministry.
- 72% of the pastors report working between 55 to 75 hours per week.
- 84% of pastors feel they are on call 24/7.
- 80% believe pastoral ministry has negatively affected their families. Many pastors' children do not attend church now because of what the church has done to their parents.

- 78% of pastors report having their vacation and personal time interrupted with ministry duties or expectations.
- 53% of pastors report that the seminary did not prepare them for the ministry.
- 90% of pastors report the ministry was completely different than what they thought it would be like before they entered the ministry.
- 57% of pastors believe they do not receive a livable wage.
- 57% of pastors report being unable to pay their bills.
- 53% of pastors are concerned about their future family financial security.
- 75% of pastors report significant stress-related crisis at least once in their ministry.
- 80% of pastors and 84% of their spouses have felt unqualified and discouraged [in the] role of pastors at least one or more times in their ministry.
- 40% report serious conflict with a parishioner at least once in the last year.
- 80% of pastors expect conflict within their church.
- Over 50% of pastors state the biggest challenge is to recruit volunteers and encourage their members to change (living closer to God's Word).[2]

2. How can I protect myself in this river—body, mind and spirit?

Physically: Over 50 percent of pastors are unhealthy and overweight and don't exercise. Here is some advice that applies to you no matter what level of ministry you are in: Make the commitment to treat your body like the temple of the Holy Spirit that it is and eat more cleanly, engage in more exercise and get more rest.

Emotionally: One statistic says 70 percent of pastors don't have someone they consider to be a close friend. Find your close friends! Whether you are in ministry or charity work, pray and ask God to send you those accountability partners whom you need.

Spiritually: Many encouraging statistics are emerging, so make sure you are among them:

- 90% of pastors feel they are called and in the place where God has called them.
- 73% of churches are treating their pastors better. This statistic has improved due to the advent of clergy appreciation, better education on the role of the pastor, and denominational awareness to better supporting their pastors.
- 77% of pastors, especially millennials (younger pastors ages usually born around 1978–1990), are spending 20 or more hours with their families each week.

Finally, spend time in daily prayer, friend. Without fail. Another statistic says 50 percent of pastors state that they spend one hour in prayer each day, and 95 percent of pastors report not praying daily or regularly with their spouse. It is impossible for you to stay full of the Holy Spirit without daily time spent in His presence. And remember, holiness is the fruit of time with Him. May we in this river never settle for the amount of the Holy Spirit we have within us, and may our fullness in Him cleanse these waters that are destined to cleanse the world.

The Coast Is Clear

How can my spiritual personality make an impact in this river?

Please note that if you are in a convergence of the ministries and charities river and another river, you will most definitely take on the following roles as a personality in that other river. But if you have both feet planted in this river, consider that you may actually fulfill the *office* and its biblical definition; therefore, we will drop the use of the word *personality* in this river.

The apostle: In the Greek, *apostolos*—"a delegate, messenger, one sent forth with orders."[3] An apostle (1) has a call to plant and oversee churches, (2) meets the same biblical qualifications of an overseer given in 1 Timothy 3:1–7, (3) has verifiable church plants and spiritual daughters and sons in the ministry, and (4) is recognized by other apostles and/or denominational boards. The Bible does not limit the designation of apostles to the twelve men chosen by Jesus. Since missionaries are of the same practical definition— "a delegate, messenger, one sent forth with orders"—both have an apostolic grace to fulfill these very duties of planting churches, overseeing sons and daughters in the faith, and brining many together just as an estuary merges rivers with the sea.

The prophet: In the Greek, *prophētēs*—"one who, moved by the Spirit of God and hence his organ or spokesman, solemnly declares to men what he has received by inspiration, especially concerning future events, and in particular such as relate to the cause and kingdom of God and to human salvation."[4] Your function is practical, although often labeled as mystical. But inscribe the words of 1 Corinthians 14:3 upon your heart: "One who prophesies speaks to men for edification and exhortation and consolation." In short, true prophecy will either build up, lift up or cheer up. This is true even when it involves the foretelling of future events, for we serve the God of hope. You are the underground river of prayer for the local church and should offer yourself to God as such for the global Church, always being faithful to release what you discern in prayer to those in authority over you.

The evangelist: In the Greek, *euangelistēs*—"a bringer of good tidings, an evangelist; the name given to the NT heralds of salvation through Christ who are not apostles."[5] Although you don't plant churches and your work is done predominantly outside the walls of the Church, you must place special emphasis on working in conjunction with local churches. As for your own personal connection, it is absolutely vital for you to be an active member of one local church that can be your home base and provide you with accountability and prayer coverage. Many a traveling evangelist has begun a ministry that started with spiritual sincerity and ended in scandal and shame. Remember that you not only have the whitewater rapids charisma to draw crowds, but you also have an anointing to dive into the enemy's whitewater rapids and rescue the drowning.

The pastor: In the Greek, *poimēn*—"a herdsman, esp. a shepherd; the presiding officer, manager, director, of any assembly: so of Christ the Head of the church."[6] Out of all five offices and personalities, please notice that this is the only one that is defined with a relationship. You are called a *shepherd*, so if you do not have a love for sheep that would cause you to choose laying down your life over self-preservation, then this position is not for you. Remember that *you* serve the Great Shepherd and that Psalm 23 tells us that He leads His sheep beside still waters. So remember that your job is to be the gentle stream that is a constant source of living water to the sheep of your flock. Hydrate them weekly with your teachings and daily with your prayers.

The teacher: In the Greek, *didaskalos*—"a teacher; in the NT one who teaches concerning the things of God, and the duties of man; one who is fitted to teach, or thinks himself so."[7] The seats of every church are full of those who think themselves to be teachers, and notice that the Greek definition of *teacher* accounts for this: "or thinks himself so." But the Word of God says, "Let not many of you become teachers, my brethren, knowing that as such we will incur a stricter judgment" (James 3:1). A true teacher is teachable. A true teacher is a student of the Word. And in a world full of scriptural misinformation, you must always be prepared to know and convey biblical truth versus popular opinion. Be guided through these waters by the Holy Spirit, one of whose names is the Spirit of Truth.

Walk on Water (from God's Word)

> When you pass through the waters, I will be with you;
> And through the rivers, they will not overflow you.
>
> Isaiah 43:2

Turn the Tide

Goals

1. For you to take your placement test to discover your river of cultural impact
2. For you to reassess your five personality types of God test from part one
3. For you to document your tests and list any convergences of cultural rivers
4. For you to find your corresponding videos and receive your commission
5. For you to work with your pastor or group to host a commissioning service

Part Three Applications

1. "Wet" Your Appetite
2. See Your Reflection
3. Plot Your Course
4. Dive In!
5. Get in the Flow

"Wet" Your Appetite

Friend, you have just waded through all twelve rivers of cultural impact in the earth today. As a result, you have also gotten a taste of nearly every occupation in all global sectors and their industries. Our hope is that you have read through each chapter entirely so you could stick your toe in each river and discover if there might be purpose there for you that you were unaware of.

Now it is time for you to return to GoMakeYourSplash.com and take your placement test to discover your river of impact. It will take you about twenty minutes, and the website will score your test for you and deliver the results to your inbox. The reason the results need to be in your inbox is so you will have easy access to this information long after you have finished this book and placed it on the shelf. That website will be full of insight for you about your occupational river and will even revisit the career paths there and link you to actual job placement websites where you can search for opportunities in your new river.

If you score very high in two different rivers of impact, then you likely will have one foot in each industry for much of your career—a convergence or "conflux." For example, both Chris and I are a conflux of the creativity river and the ministry river. (But I also play around quite a bit in the entertainment river!)

Perhaps you are already sure of your river of impact and won't be at all surprised at the outcome of your placement test. Whatever the case, it is time for new experiences in your river as you learn to flow in it with new purpose.

So head now to GoMakeYourSplash.com and click on Rivers Test!

See Your Reflection

In part one, you learned that God has five distinct personality types through which He reveals Himself to the world very relationally: the apostle personality, the prophet personality, the evangelist personality, the pastor personality and the teacher personality. Then you saw examples of Jesus flowing in each of these personality types during His ministry, and even flowing in and out of them during one conversation!

Then you took a test at the GoMakeYourSplash.com website to discover your primary spiritual personality, and you even learned if you are a hybrid of two or more of them. (For example, I am a hybrid of the pastor personality and the apostle personality. Laura is a hybrid of the prophet personality and the teacher personality.)

Later in part one, you explored what type of conversations these spiritual personalities might engage in. Hopefully, you also learned a bit about how you have processed thoughts and speech your whole life.

Then in part two, you studied all twelve global sectors or rivers, including their occupations and industries. There, all the odd jobs from your past and the occupational dreams for your future came together to help you make sense of where you are headed in your particular river of influence. Having all this information—which is a vital key to unlocking your life, your walk and your career—you will now have an idea of what it will look like to be used by God in that industry, and you can picture yourself in it, interacting with others for maximum impact. Also remember that you will now be faced with two options: sink or swim. And to know *HOW* to do that is to do it the *"Holy Only Way,"* employing the fruits of the Spirit listed in Galatians 5. Then and only then will you see Christ's reflection when you look into the waters, and then and only then will others who are watching see Him in you.

Plot Your Course

Congratulations! You have made three important discoveries about yourself through the various forms and tests in this book. You have discovered your net worth, your spiritual personality and your river of influence. Now, in this section, you will make the application where you start plotting your course. To help with that, you are going to briefly list your results to get an overview of who you are and where you go from here.

From your part one "net worth" work sheet, list your natural and acquired gifts here:

From your part one spiritual personality test, list your results here:

From your part two study of the twelve rivers of cultural impact, list your first impressions of what your primary river or occupational industry is, also noting any suspected convergences:

_____

_____

_____

From your part three rivers placement test, list the generated results here of your river of impact and any convergences with other rivers:

_____

_____

_____

_____

Dive In!

We want to pray over you, bless you and commission you into your river of impact. Go to GoMakeYourSplash.com and click on Commissioning Videos. From there, click on your river of impact:

 Home and Family

 Information Technology

 Healthcare and Therapeutic Sciences

 Politics and Law

 Military and Paramilitary

 Creativity

Entertainment and Recreation

Consumer Services and Commerce

 Academics and Training

Press and Telecommunications

Energy and Utilities

Ministries and Charities

And now, for a video prayer of blessing over your spiritual personality, visit GoMakeYourSplash.com and click on Personality Blessing.

Get in the Flow

Friend, it has been our privilege to be your tour guides on this river adventure through all of God's amazing rivers of impact. We hope it has convinced you that not only has He given you a purpose, but that you are also the only one who can fulfill it. What will happen in your river of impact if you never jump in? Or what will happen if you jump in but stay silent? And worst of all, what would happen if you eventually went under?

Now there is no longer any need for fear, hesitancy or silence. You have "wetted" your appetite, seen your reflection (and Christ's) in the water, plotted your course, and now you are diving in headfirst and getting in the flow! But we want to encourage you to find other believers who belong in your river of impact so you can journey together and experience greater accountability, companionship and encouragement along the way.

The best way to do this is for your entire church or company to host a Go Make Your Splash commissioning service, as we did at Eastgate Creative Christian Fellowship. Or you could plan a Go Make Your Splash weekend event where you go through the entire book, along with taking its tests. There is nothing like sitting with like-minded kindred spirits and coming alive with purpose to impact your industry!

In the previous application, you watched a video that commissioned you into your river of impact. Now we have another video for you that will give you a taste of what a commissioning service and Go Make Your Splash weekend should look like in your church, place of business, club or small group. Once again, visit GoMakeYourSplash.com and click on Experience a Go Make Your Splash Commissioning Service! We urge you to send this link to your pastor or employer. Or if you already are the pastor or employer, we urge you to make this a priority for the people whom you lead.

We are available to answer your questions at info@GoMake YourSplash.com, and you can even invite us both in to perform your commissioning service for you. We can also host a complete Go Make Your Splash event at your church or company. For more details, please visit the GoMakeYourSplash.com website.

High in the sky
where birds do fly
is where clouds form
And God does try . . .

. . . to shower His earth
each person of birth
with purpose and passion
and show them their worth.

Through mountains grand
and from His hand
the droplets are falling
each one with a plan.

Each raindrop is different
each cold snowflake too.
They hit the ground running;
they're headed for you.

Through Estuary alleys
and Underground valleys
His plan rushes in as
the Whitewater rallies.

As the Gentle Stream threads
and each Tributary spreads
His purpose hits earth
filling each riverbed

Through all populations
they outsource the nations;
where commerce meets calling
in all generations.

So, quick as a flash
just make a mad dash.
There's impact inside you,
so go make your splash!

© Chris and Laura Smith
April 30, 2022

Notes

Chapter 6 Born of Water and Spirit

1. Blue Letter Bible, s.v. "qadas" (Strong's H6942), https://www.blueletterbible .org/lexicon/h6942/nasb95/wlc/0-1.
2. Blue Letter Bible, s.v. "natan" (Strong's H5414), https://www.blueletterbible .org/lexicon/h5414/nasb95/wlc/0-1.

Chapter 7 Uncharted Waters

1. Wikipedia, s.v. "River," last modified March 30, 2022, https://en.wikipedia .org/wiki/River.
2. Wikipedia, s.v. "Stream," last modified February 6, 2022, https:// en.wikipedia.org/a/Stream.
3. Wikipedia, s.v. "Subterranean river," last modified January 13, 2022, https:// en.wikipedia.org/wiki/Subterranean_river.
4. Wikipedia, s.v. "Tributary," last modified February 13, 2022, https:// en.wikipedia.org/wiki/Tributary.
5. Wikipedia, s.v. "Whitewater," last modified November 2, 2021, https:// en.wikipedia.org/wiki/Whitewater.
6. Wikipedia, s.v. "Estuaries," last modified March 29, 2022, https:// en.wikipedia.org/wiki/Estuary.

Chapter 8 Go with the Flow

1. These Greek word definitions all come from Blue Letter Bible's online lexicon. In chapter 22, we will give you even more specific definitions for each word when we talk about how your spiritual personality can affect the river of influence you are in. We will also provide notes about where you can find each definition online if you'd like to study it yourself.

Chapter 9 Come On In, the Water's Fine!

1. For more information on my online creative writing class, go to Laura HarrisSmith.com/writingprogram.

2. Lois Zoppi, B.A., "What Makes Different People More or Less Susceptible to Altitude Sickness?" New Medical Life Sciences, May 21, 2021, https://www.n ews-medical.net/health/What-Makes-Different-People-More-or-Less-Susceptible -to-Altitude-Sickness.aspx.

3. Joshua C. Tremblay and Philip N. Ainslie, "Global and country-level estimates of human population at high altitude," National Library of Medicine, April 26, 2021, https://www.ncbi.nlm.nih.gov/pmc/articles/PMC8106311.

Chapter 16 Home and Family River

1. This and the other statistics in this paragraph are from Natalie Bogdanski, "Are Divorce Rates in the U.S. on the Rise?," updated January 21, 2022, https:// www.divorcemag.com/blog/are-divorce-rates-in-the-u-s-on-the-rise.

Chapter 12 Information Technology River

1. Erik Gregerson, "History of Technology Timeline," Encyclopaedia Britannica Inc., ©2022, https://www.britannica.com/story/history-of-technology-timeline.

2. Jonah Comstock, "Lumo: 60 percent of workers have tech-related health problems," mobihealthnews.com, October 10, 2013, https://www.mobihealth news.com/26207/lumo-60-percent-of-workers-have-tech-related-health -problems.

3. Ibid.

4. Ibid.

Chapter 13 Healthcare and Therapeutic Sciences River

1. Drew DeSilver, "10 facts about American workers," Pew Research Center, August 29, 2019, https://www.pewresearch.org/fact-tank/2019/08/29/facts-about -american-workers.

2. Bobby Joseph, and Merlyn Joseph, "The health of the healthcare workers," National Library of Medicine, May–August 20, 2016, https://www.ncbi.nlm.nih .gov/pmc/articles/PMC5299814.

3. "The Critical Health Impacts of Corruption," National Library of Medi-cine, 2018, https://www.ncbi.nlm.nih.gov/books/NBK535646.

4. Ibid.

5. Steven Bedard, Anna Fort, Elaine Gottlieb, Michael Laker, Cynthia A. McKeown, Christopher Riegle, and Arthur R. Smith (content producers), "Sleep, Performance, and Public Safety," Division of Sleep Medicine at Harvard Medical School, December 18, 2007, http://healthysleep.med.harvard.edu/healthy/matters /consequences/sleep- performance-and-public-safety.

6. WordSense Dictionary, s.v. "docent," https://www.wordsense.eu/docent/.

Chapter 14 Politics and Law River

1. Evan Andrews, "8 Things You May Not Know About Hammurabi's Code," History Channel online, last updated August 31, 2018, https://www.history.com /news/8-things-you-may-not-know-about-hammurabis-code.

2. "New study on lawyer well-being reveals serious concerns for legal profession," the American Bar Association (ABA), December 2017, https://www.americ anbar.org/news/abanews/publications/youraba/2017/december-2017/secrecy-and -fear-of-stigma-among-the-barriers-to-lawyer-well-bei.

3. Ibid.

4. Nicolas Tomboulides, "Congress: Too Many Lawyers and Lifelong Politicians," May 13, 2020, https://www.termlimits.com/occupational-hazard-lack-of -professional-diversity-in-congress.

Chapter 15 Military and Paramilitary River

1. Blue Letter Bible, s.v. "shamar" (Strong's H8104), https://www.blueletter bible.org/lexicon/h8104/nasb95/wlc/0-1.

2. "Army Injuries, Causes, Risk Factors, and Prevention Overview," Army Public Health Center (APHC), last updated March 14, 2022, https://phc.amedd .army.mil/topics/discond/ptsaip/Pages/Army-Injuries-Causes-Risk-Factors-and -Prevention-Overview.aspx.

3. Audrey A. Reichard, and Larry L. Jackson, "Occupational injuries among emergency responders," National Library of Medicine, January 2010, https:// pubmed.ncbi.nlm.nih.gov/19894221.

4. PTSD: "How Common is PTSD in Veterans?" National Center for PTSD, U.S. Department of Veterans Affairs, https://www.ptsd.va.gov/understand/common /common_veterans.asp.

Chapter 16 Creativity River (Fine Arts and Intellectual Property)

1. Eniola Alabi, *Racially Influenced Witchcraft: A Biblical Perspective* (London: Enitonni Publishing, 2003), 25–26. See also https://www.google.com/book s/edition/Racially_Influenced_Witchcraft/ChuF9N0ZtrgC?hl=en&gbpv=1&d q=Frances+frangipane+just+one+minor+demonic+influence&pg=PA26&pr intsec=frontcover.

2. Nadra Nittle, "The Link Between Depression and Creativity," Verywell Mind, last updated February 5, 2021, https://www.verywellmind.com/the-link -between-depression-and-creativity-5094193.

Chapter 17 Entertainment and Recreation River

1. *Merriam-Webster Dictionary*, s.v. "entertainment," Merriam-Webster online, https://www.merriam-webster.com/dictionary/entertainment.

2. Michael Kaliszewski, Ph.D., reviewer, "The Entertainment Industry and Addiction in America," American Addiction Centers, March 15, 2022, https:// americanaddictioncenters.org/blog/entertainments-influence-on-addiction.

3. Kara Ladd, and Victoria Sines, "55 Celebrities Who Don't Drink Alcohol," December 13, 2021, *Harper's Bazaar* online, https://www.harpersbazaar.com/celebrity /latest/g11644970/celebrities-who-dont-drink-alcohol/?slide=50.

4. Tim Fitzgerald, "Professional Athletes," HealthDay online, December 31, 2020, https://consumer.healthday.com/encyclopedia/work-and-health-41/occup ational-health-news-507/professional-athletes-648171.html.

5. Ibid.

6. *Merriam-Webster Dictionary*, s.v. "celebrity," *Merriam-Webster* online, https://www.merriam-webster.com/dictionary/celebrity.

Chapter 18 Consumer Services and Commerce River

1. "Workplace Stress: A Silent Killer of Employee Health and Productivity," *Corporate Wellness Magazine* online, https://www.corporatewellnessmagazine .com/article/workplace-stress-silent-killer-employee-health-productivity.

2. Ibid.

3. Ibid.

4. Ibid.

Chapter 19 Academics and Training River

1. Melanie Hanson, "Average Cost Of College And Tuition," last updated June 12, 2022, Education Data Initiative, https://educationdata.org/average -cost-of-college.

2. "A Look at the Shocking Student Loan Debt Statistics for 2022," Student Loan Hero: Lending Tree (data via the Federal Reserve, College Board and Saving for College), last updated April 6, 2022, https://studentloanhero.com/student-loan -debt-statistics.

3. Chris Parr, "Top 5 major economies with 'corrupt' education systems," October 4, 2013, https://www.timeshighereducation.com/features/top-5-major -economies-with-corrupt-education-systems/2007926.article.

4. "Education Rankings by Country 2022" (from a Best Countries report), World Population Review, https://worldpopulationreview.com/country-rankings /education-rankings-by-country.

5. Ibid.

6. "Homeschool Statistics," Time 4 Learning, https://www.time4learning.com /homeschool/homeschoolstatistics.shtml.

7. M. T. Greenberg, J. L. Brown, and R. M. Abenavoli, "Teacher Stress and Health," Pennsylvania State University, September 1, 2016, https://www.rwjf.org /en/library/research/2016/07/teacher-stress-and-health.html.

8. Vaneetha Rendall Risner, "Will You Lose Your Faith in College?," Desiring God ministry online, August 23. 2018, https://www.desiringgod.org/articles/will -you-lose-your-faith-in-college.

Chapter 20 Press and Telecommunications River

1. John Naisbitt, *Megatrends: Ten New Directions Transforming Our Lives* (New York: Warner Books, 1982), n.p.

2. Sabine Heim, and Andreas Keil, "Too Much Information, Too Little Time: How the Brain Separates Important from Unimportant Things in Our Fast-Paced Media World," Frontiers for Young Minds, June 1, 2017, https://kids.frontiersin .org/articles/10.3389/frym.2017.00023.

Chapter 21 Energy and Utilities River

1. Dr. Knowledge, "How much energy does the sun produce?," Globe Newspaper Company, September 5, 2005, http://archive.boston.com/news/science/articles /2005/09/05/how_much_energy_does_the_sun_produce.

2. Office of Nuclear Energy, "Nuclear Power Is the Most Reliable Energy Source and It's Not Even Close," Energy.gov, March 24, 2021, https://www.energy.gov/ne/ articles/nuclear-power-most-reliable-energy-source-and-its-not-even-close.

3. Ibid.

4. Kiwi Energy, "Pros and Cons of Nuclear Energy," last updated March 24, 2021, https://kiwienergy.us/pros-and-cons-of-nuclear-energy.

5. Steven Bedard, Anna Fort, Elaine Gottlieb, Michael Laker, Cynthia A. McKeown, Christopher Riegle, and Arthur R. Smith (content producers), "Sleep, Performance, and Public Safety," Division of Sleep Medicine at Harvard Medical School, December 18, 2007, http://healthysleep.med.harvard.edu/healthy/matters /consequences/sleep-performance-and-public-safety.

6. Bectu, "Health and safety in the energy sector," bectu.org.uk, 2021, https:// bectu.org.uk/health-and-safety-in-the-energy-sector.

7. Ibid.

8. "On-Site Safety in the Power and Utilities Industry," Mobile Medical Corporation, https://www.mobmed.com/occupational-health-solutions/utilities-and -power.

9. Ibid.

Chapter 22 Ministries and Charities River

1. "Statistics in the Ministry," PastoralCareInc.com, © 2022, https://www .pastoralcareinc.com/statistics.

2. Once again, these statistics and those that follow are from the article I mentioned that you can find, along with some discussion and clarification of the various stats, at https://www.pastoralcareinc.com/statistics.

3. Blue Letter Bible, s.v. "apostolos" (Strong's G652), https://www.blueletter bible.org/lexicon/g652/nasb95/mgnt/0-1.

4. Blue Letter Bible., s.v. "prophētēs" (Strong's G4396), https://www.blueletter bible.org/lexicon/g4396/nasb95/mgnt/0-1.

5. Blue Letter Bible, s.v. "euangelistēs" (Strong's G2099), https://www.blueletter bible.org/lexicon/g2099/nasb95/mgnt/0-1.

6. Blue Letter Bible, s.v. "poimēn" (Strong's G4166), https://www.blueletter bible.org/lexicon/g4166/nasb95/mgnt/0-1.

7. Blue Letter Bible, s.v. "didaskalos" (Strong's G1320), https://www.blueletter bible.org/lexicon/g1320/nasb95/mgnt/0-1.

Dr. Christopher Lee Smith founded Eastgate Creative Christian Fellowship in Nashville with Laura, and they have pastored there for almost 20 years. Together, they are the presidents of Eastgate Christian College, an online accredited college that issues associate's, bachelor's, master's and doctoral degrees in media, nutrition, biblical studies and worshiping arts (EastgateChristianCollege.com). Before his call to ministry, Chris spent more than 30 successful years in producing, songwriting, publishing and artist development. He represented music by The Beatles, Elton John, Amy Grant, Third Day, Unspoken and more. He and Laura live near Nashville. Visit EastgateCCF.com for more details.

Dr. Laura Harris Smith is a naturopathic doctor with four degrees in original medicine. She is the CEO of Neuromatics Oil and inventor of its three patented healing oil blends: Quiet Brain, Happy Brain and Sharp Brain. (Visit NeuromaticsOil.com to see all her health products available there.) Laura is also the host of her popular faith-based TV talk show *theTHREE*. With over 50 years of experience onstage and on-screen, she has authored more than 25 books. She and Chris have 6 children and 14 grandchildren, and they hate it when everyone goes home after movie night. Visit LauraHarrisSmith.com to view all of Laura's books and resources.

Eastgate Creative Christian Fellowship is an interdenominational community of Christian believers in Nashville, Tennessee, who love God's Word, worship in spirit and in truth, serve the community, and whom you can call family even if you have never had any denominational affiliation. They'd love to have you at the family table every Sunday starting at 10 a.m. at their facility at 633 Shute Lane, Old Hickory, Tennessee, 37138. Eastgate also has small groups that meet almost every day of the week in various locations across the city. To watch their services online, go to EastgateCCF.com and click on "Livestream." Also visit that website for more information on the church, the staff, their statement of faith and associated ministries.

You can invite Chris and Laura to come host a Make Your Splash event by contacting them here:

Make Your Splash Bookings: bookings@GoMakeYourSplash.com

Chris: chris@EastgateCCF.com

Laura: bookings@LauraHarrisSmith.com

More from Laura Harris Smith

With absorbing insight, *Seeing the Voice of God* demystifies nighttime dreams and daytime visions, revealing the science behind the supernatural and giving you a biblical foundation for making sense of what you see. Includes a comprehensive Dream Symbols Dictionary with over 1,000 biblical definitions.

Seeing the Voice of God

Invisible faith toxins can cause symptoms that affect our entire being—mind, body and spirit. In this one-month detox, expert Laura Harris Smith uncovers thirty faith toxins and promotes biblical healing of the whole person through prayer, Scripture and simple recipes. Refresh and refuel yourself spiritually, mentally and physically with this practical guide.

The 30-Day Faith Detox

Accessible, practical and grounded in real life, *The Healthy Living Handbook* is full of simple everyday ways to live a truly healthy life—body, mind and spirit. These easy-to-implement lifestyle tips will not only bring the peace, rest, energy, connection and clarity you've been longing for, but help you to live better in every area of life.

The Healthy Living Handbook

You May Also Like . . .

Studies show that sleep plays a vital role in reducing stress, lowering health risks and increasing productivity. But what happens when you simply *can't* sleep? Laura Harris Smith will make you aware of the harmful spiritual, emotional and physical effects of what is keeping you awake and lead you to a place of peace where you will learn to hear God speak.

Give It to God and Go to Bed

Chosen

 Stay up to date on your favorite books and authors with our free e-newsletters. Sign up today at chosenbooks.com.

 facebook.com/chosenbooks

@chosen_books